WORLD BIBLIOGRAPHICAL SERIES

General Editors:
Robert L. Collison (Editor-in-chief)
Sheila R. Herstein
Louis J. Reith
Hans H. Wellisch

VOLUME 8

Malawi

Robert B. Boeder

Lecturer in History,
University of Malawi

Malawi

CLIO PRESS

OXFORD, ENGLAND · SANTA BARBARA, CALIFORNIA

British Library Cataloguing in Publication Data

Boeder, Robert B
    Malawi – (World bibliographical series; vol. 8).
    1. Malawi – Bibliography
    I. Title II. Series
    016.9689'7   Z3577

ISBN 0-903450-22-4

Designed by Bernard Crossland
Computer typeset by Peter Peregrinus Ltd.
Printed in Great Britain
by T. & A. Constable Ltd., Edinburgh

Clio Press Ltd.,
Woodside House, Hinksey Hill,
Oxford OX1 5BE, England.
Providing the services of the European
Bibliographical Centre and the American
Bibliographical Center.

American Bibliographical Center-Clio Press,
Riviera Campus, 2040 Alameda Padre Serra,
Santa Barbara, Ca. 93103, U.S.A.

To the memory of James R. Hooker,
Malawianist, teacher and friend

Contents

Contents

Introduction

While researching and writing this annotated bibliography I kept thinking about the great distance that Malawi and its people have travelled in the country's century and a quarter of written history – the country has developed from an area devastated by the slave trade and warlike invaders to an independent nation with a thriving agricultural economy. Equally amazing are the strange and wonderful people who have written about this beautiful part of southeastern Africa. Books and articles have been published by African slave boys who later became Anglican priests; by brilliant British medical doctors who, sick of Western ways, became recluses living alone among their African friends; and by brave women who undertook solitary journeys of a thousand miles or more through the bush nearly a century ago.

Perhaps one reason Malawi has attracted such 'characters' is that it is something of a maverick itself. As a nation-state it has gone its own way in Southern Africa by stressing hard work, agricultural development, pragmatic no-nonsense politics, and a form of mixed economy which has welcomed outside investment and achieved considerable success. Alone among its neighbours Malawi is able to feed itself. Since independence, exports have grown fourfold, real per capita income and the annual budget have doubled, and British monetary assistance has been eliminated. The country is censored by many for trading openly with South Africa (while its critics do so in private), but international loan and development experts consider Malawi a model example of how a young country can progress if its leadership is clear-sighted and its people apply themselves.

This volume is intended as a reference work for the public. There are over 1,000 items listed: 50 theses and dissertations, over 550 numbered and annotated entries, and 450 additional works mentioned within the annotations. However, it cannot be called comprehensive, and graduate students will still need to do their own in-depth research. Nevertheless, the present work is quite detailed, particularly in well-developed disciplines such as history and religion, which exemplify the richness of written material in English on Malawi. It is

Introduction

incomplete in such areas as education, where previous bibliographies have been done, and in addition only a few published government reports are mentioned. Similarly, I have not recorded every item by or about David Livingstone, both because the amount of material on his life is so vast that it requires a separate bibliography and because much of what has been produced is irrelevant to Malawi. Various University of Malawi faculty members are working on detailed bibliographies covering their particular subject areas, and perhaps in five years' time it will be possible to publish an annotated work which can claim to be comprehensive.

While compiling this work my impression has been that, in broad general terms, the written literature on Malawi can be divided in one of two ways. The first approach is to say that up to 1910 and after 1950 there was a tremendous amount of writing, but that not much appeared in between. In particular, it seems as though everyone who set foot in British Central Africa before 1910 felt compelled to write about it. The second approach is to divide the literature into three chronological categories. First came the missionaries and those around them, the traders, and government officials, all of whom wrote about their own work, as well as books about travel and exploration, from 1860 to 1930. Next came the anthropologists, biologists and geographers, who produced works of value from 1930 to 1960. Around that time the historians (of whom I am one) took over, and they are still going strong.

Connecting the three periods have been 'bridge' individuals working in two or more disciplines such as the missionary/anthropologist T. Cullen Young in the late 1920s and the anthropologist/historian Matthew Schoffeleers in the 1960s. This division will undoubtedly be far too simple for some, and I hope it prompts reviewers' comments, but one constant has remained: the domination of writing about Malawi by Scots or people of Scots descent. The index is full of Macdonalds, McCrakens, Macmillans, Stewarts (and one Stuart), Kerrs, and Scotts. It is remarkable that a country small enough to fit inside the circumference of Lake Malawi has had such an enormous influence on the land around the lake. It is said that the first educated Malawians who emigrated to work in South Africa could hardly be understood because they spoke English with impenetrable Scots accents picked up from their Blantyre and Livingstonia Mission teachers. One can even identify a kind of 'Scottish mafia' of Scots Presbyterian laymen and pastors who defend early missionary efforts in their writings, and of trained historians who could be more critical about early Scottish trading activities in

Introduction

Central Africa. That 'the Scots stick together' is certainly true in Malawi.

There have been other links between the authors of Malawiana. One link has been between history and language or linguistics, and Dr. Banda, T. Cullen Young, W. A. Elmslie, and Leroy Vail have all made contributions in both active and academic ways. Also, thankfully, there have always been women writing about the country, and Malawians themselves have figured prominently in their country's historiography over the decades. Another important contribution has been that of medical doctors. They, especially, have written about British Central Africa, while helping to mould it into its present form, Livingstone, Poole, Laws, Elmslie, James Johnston, James Stewart, John Kirk, G. M. Sanderson, Michael Gelfand, Daniel Malekebu and Dr. Banda, to name only a few, have published writings, but curiously little has been done on Malawian medicine, either modern or traditional.

There are other blank spots awaiting chroniclers. Despite all the historical literature, even in such minor areas as postal history, there is still no competent economic history of the country nor is there a first-rate history of African agriculture – perhaps because no one has yet appeared with the special gifts and experience required to write one. For the precolonial period, clan histories are needed and also examinations of the pre-Bantu Akafula peoples.

There have been numerous studies of Protestant missions. The Universities' Mission to Central Africa in particular has published a vast amount of literature about itself, but until recently, with the work of Schoffeleers and Linden, no comparable histories have been done of Catholic missions and their effects on the country and its people. Catholic priests kept diaries of their daily lives and mission events and wrote treatises about local customs, but often these were in French or German and were not made public for fear of annoying the British colonial authorities.

Early independent churchmen like John Chilembwe have been thoroughly studied, but little light has been thrown on the activities of religious separatists since independence. In addition, Islam in Malawi still requires further research. Most scholars (and I am no different myself) prefer to remain in their dusty libraries and archives working out new angles on old topics, taking previous writers to task for ignoring minor points, and arguing endlessly over trivia; but it takes gifted, active people prepared to go into the field to open up a research area such as Islam. Likewise, a true military history of Malawi, describing the defeats as well as the victories, has yet to be

Introduction

written. And although most of the country's ethnic groups have been well covered, one, the Lomwe, has been neglected. Again, halfway through my research I found myself wondering whatever happened to the Tonga; during the 1950s there was a burst of interest in this group, mainly due to the vigour of Jaap van Velsen, but since then no follow-up studies have been done.

External labour migration has been adequately researched, but internal migration has not, and the entire plantation/estate system, especially where labour is concerned, remains to be investigated. A complete study is also needed of the slave trade in British Central Africa, and its role in precolonial economies and social and political systems.

A political history of Malawi since independence has yet to be attempted. Studies should be done of the Malawi Congress Party, the Young Pioneers, the role of the League of Malawi Women, and ethnicity in politics, but these are sensitive issues and for one reason or another scholars will have to wait. For 'nationalist' historiography has been replaced by more fashionable 'class' historiography and by studies of underdevelopment. However, an examination of the role of trade unions in the independence struggle could be undertaken if official approval was forthcoming.

There have been flocks of ardent bird watchers in Malawi over the years, keeping faithful scores of their sightings, and much has been written about the charm of the Nyika Plateau, although surprisingly little has been done on Mount Mulanje or Zomba Plateau.

As for individuals, Dr. Malekebu is probably the most neglected 20th century figure. John Chilembwe's successor at Providence Industrial Mission, an MD and ordained minister, he has stayed in the background, and remained content to mind his own business while others hold the limelight. Some of the work on early missionaries and explorers requires a more objective reconsideration, and the nearly forgotten Blantyre Mission scandal of the late 1870s needs reexamination.

Let me say a final word about recent developments in Malawian literature, and especially about the appearance since independence of a popular culture centring around the *Nyau* secret society. When I first arrived in Malawi in 1964, the *Nyau* were still a dynamic part of everyday life. The people living around the mission station where I was teaching in Central Region believed in *Nyau* and guarded its secrets closely. Since then much has been written about the *Nyau*, and in the process it seems as if the mystery, romance and vitality of the *Nyau* in Cewa society have been lost. Perhaps I am exaggerating, and

xii

Introduction

perhaps this is the inevitable result of moving into the 20th century, but with *Nyau* masks on sale in public and the dances being performed for large audiences – with even Europeans joining in – something has been lost. Perhaps to popularize a culture is to destroy it. Two final notes. Firstly, in this volume Malawi is also referred to as British Central Africa, Nyasaland, the Protectorate, and the land of the lake. Secondly, in numerous instances throughout this work I have cited individual essays taken from edited collections of essays. In these cases I have included in the bibliographical details of each essay a reference to the edited work, full details of which are provided in an entry for the book as a whole elsewhere in the volume. Collections treated in this fashion include *From Nyasaland to Malawi*, edited by R. Macdonald, and *Malawi: the history of a nation*, edited by Bridglal Pachai.

In collecting my materials I had the assistance of librarians at Michigan State University, the British Museum, the Commonwealth Society, the University of London, the University of Edinburgh and its Centre for African Studies, the University of Zambia Special Collections, the University of Malawi and its Malawi Collection, and the library of the National Archives in Zomba. I borrowed liberally from the annotated bibliography in Murlene McKinnon's dissertation on lake and river transportation, and my thanks are also due to Mr. Peter Turner for his help. Responsibility for all errors, either of commission or omission, is mine.

Lusaka
September 1978

xiii

Place names in Malawi

The following list of place name alterations appeared in the *Government Gazette* from time to time up to 1975.

Former Name	New Name
Cholo	Thyolo
Deep Bay	Chirumba
Florence Bay	Chitimba
Fort Hill	Chitipa
Fort Johnston	Mangochi
Fort Manning	Mchinji
Kochira	Kochirira
Kota Kota	Nkhotakota
Lake Nyasa	Lake Malawi
Lufilya	Lufira
Malosa	Muloza
Mkhoma	Nkhoma
Mlanje	Mulanje
Murchison Falls	Kholombidzo Falls
Nkata Bay	Nkhata Bay
Ntakataka	Mtakataka
Ntondwe	Thondwe
Palombe	Phalombe
Port Herald	Nsanje
Rumpi	Rumphi
Tuchila	Thuchila
Vipya	Viphya
Visanza	Ntchisi

Theses and dissertations on Malawi

Edward Alter Alpers. 'The role of the Yao in the development of trade in East-Central Africa', PhD thesis, University of London, 1966.

Timothy Kiel Barnekov. 'An inquiry into the development of native administration in Nyasaland, 1888–1939', MA thesis, San Jose State College, California.

Keith Bloomfield. 'The petrology of the basement complex in part of southern Nyasaland with particular reference to infracrustal rocks', PhD thesis, Leeds University, 1963.

Robert Benson Boeder. 'Malawians abroad: a history of labor emigration from Malawi to its neighbours, 1890 to the present', PhD dissertation, Michigan State University, 1974.

Bruce P. Browne. 'A politico-geographical analysis of Malawi's borderlands', MA thesis, Michigan State University, 1972.

Martin Leon Chanock. 'British policy in Central Africa, 1908–1926', PhD thesis, University of Cambridge, 1968.

Aleck Humphrey Che-Mponda. 'The Malawi–Tanzania border and territorial dispute, 1968: a case study of boundary and territorial imperatives in the new Africa', PhD dissertation, Howard University, 1972.

Cynthia Ann Crosby. 'A history of the Nyasaland Railway, 1895–1935: a study in colonial economic development', PhD dissertation, Syracuse University, 1974.

Cyril Vernon Cutting. 'Chemical aspects of some Nyasaland soils with reference to the production of tung oil and tea', PhD thesis, University of London, 1956.

Ronald E. Gregson. 'Work, exchange and leadership: the mobilization of agricultural labor among the Tumbuka of the Henga Valley', PhD dissertation, Columbia University, 1969.

Bernard Anderton Harawa. 'The Teachers' Union of Malawi: its emergence, development and activities from 1943 to 1973', EdD dissertation, Columbia University, 1974.

Deborah Ann Harding. 'The phonology and morphology of Chinyanja', PhD thesis, UCLA, 1966.

Theses and dissertations on Malawi

Trevor Hill. 'The phonetics of a Nyanja speaker', MA thesis, University of London, 1948.

Jacob Ogbonnaya Ibik. 'Law of marriage in Nyasaland', PhD thesis, University of London, 1966.

Leslie Austin Lionel James. 'Education in the Rhodesias and Nyasaland, 1890–1963', PhD dissertation, New York University, 1965.

Selby Hickey Joffe. 'Political culture and communication in Malawi: the hortatory regime of Kamuzu Banda', PhD dissertation, Boston University, 1973.

Zemani David Kadzamira. 'Local politics and the administration of development in Malawi', PhD thesis, University of Manchester, 1974.

Owen J. Kalinga. 'The Ngonde kingdom of northern Malawi, 1600–1895', PhD thesis, University of London, 1974.

J.A.K. Kandawire. 'Local leadership and socio-economic changes in Chingale area of Zomba district in Malawi', PhD thesis, University of Edinburgh, 1972.

S. Kaye. 'The role of agriculture in Malawi', BA thesis, University of Natal, 1972.

Korn Irving Leslie Kornfield. 'Evolutionary genetics of endemic Cichlid fishes (Pisces: Cichlidae) in Lake Malawi, Africa', PhD dissertation, SUNY at Stony Brook, 1974.

B. S. Krishnamurthy. 'Land and labour in Nyasaland, 1891–1914', PhD thesis, University of London, 1964.

Harold Marius Lange. 'The development of higher education in an emergent country: Malawi, Africa, 1960–1967', EdD dissertation, University of Southern California, 1973.

Harry Wells Langworthy. 'A history of Undi's kingdom to 1890; aspects of Chewa history in East Central Africa', PhD dissertation, Boston University, 1969.

D. H. Laycock. 'Experiments in the growing and harvesting of tea in Nyasaland', MSc thesis, University of Leeds, 1955.

Roderick J. Macdonald. 'A history of African education in Nyasaland, 1875–1945', PhD dissertation, University of Edinburgh, 1969.

William Eugene Mackie. 'Radio broadcasting in Malawi: a search for identity and service', PhD dissertation, University of Missouri, 1971.

Murlene McKinnon. 'Commerce, Christianity and the gunboat: an historical study of Malawi lake and river transport, 1850–1914', PhD dissertation, Michigan State University, 1977.

Hugh W. Macmillan. 'The origins and development of the African Lakes Company: 1878–1908', PhD thesis, University of Edinburgh, 1970.

Theses and dissertations on Malawi

Emily Nyamazao Maliwa. 'The history of nationalism and intellectual movements in Nyasaland', MA thesis, University of Chicago, 1961.

Emily Nyamazao Maliwa. 'Customary law and administration of justice, 1890–1933', MPhil dissertation, University of London, 1967.

J. A. C. Mapanje. 'The use of traditional literary forms in modern Malawian writing in English', MPhil thesis, University of London, 1975.

D. Milazi. 'Malawian migration in relation to the South African farming and mining economy', PhD dissertation, Free University of West Berlin, 1975.

Kenneth W. Mufuka. 'The role of a missionary in the colonization of Malawi, 1875–1927: an assessment of the career of Dr. Robert Laws', MA thesis, University of St. Andrews, 1971.

Steve S. Mwiyeriwa. 'Vernacular literature of Malawi, 1854–1975, an annotated bibliography', FLA thesis, 1978.

C. R. Namponya. 'Agriculture in Malawi: an annotated bibliography, 1930–1974', FLA thesis, 1976.

D. Nkhwazi. 'Presidential leadership in Malawi', PhD dissertation, University of Hamburg, 1971.

G. T. Nurse. 'The physical characters of the Maravi', PhD thesis, University of Witwatersrand, 1975.

Melvin E. Page. 'Malawians in the Great War and after, 1914–1925', PhD dissertation, Michigan State University, 1977.

Kings M. Phiri. 'Chewa history in central Malawi and the use of oral tradition', PhD dissertation, University of Wisconsin, 1975.

Simon Arthur Roberts. 'The growth of an integrated legal system in Malawi: a study in racial distinctions in the law', PhD thesis, University of London, 1967.

Andrew C. Ross. 'Origins and development of the Church of Scotland Mission, Blantyre, Nyasaland, 1875–1926', PhD thesis, University of Edinburgh, 1968.

F. E. Sanderson. 'Nyasaland migrant labour in British Central Africa, 1890–1939', MA thesis, Manchester University, 1960.

Matthew Schoffeleers. 'Symbolic and social aspects of spirit worship among the Mang'anja', PhD thesis, Oxford University, 1968.

Matthew Schoffeleers. 'M'bona the guardian spirit of the Mang'anja', BLitt thesis, Oxford University, 1966.

Richard G. Stuart. 'Christianity and the Chewa: the Anglican case, 1885–1950', PhD thesis, University of London, 1974.

Roger Tangri. 'The development of modern African politics and

Theses and dissertations on Malawi

emergence of a nationalist movement in colonial Malawi', PhD thesis, University of Edinburgh, 1970.

Leroy Vail. 'Aspects of the Tumbuka verb', PhD dissertation, University of Wisconsin.

Betty Wilbert. 'Education in Malawi', MA thesis, Howard University, 1965.

David Wilson. 'The improvement of basic data used in educational planning: a case study – Malawi', PhD dissertation, Syracuse University, 1969.

The Country and its People

1 **Blantyre District.**
Colin A. Baker. *Nyasaland Journal*, vol. 12, pt. 1 (Jan.
1959), p. 7-35.
This article traces the growth of the Blantyre District, describing the distribution
and composition of its African population against the physical and cultural background of the area.

2 **The Shire Highlands, East Central Africa, as colony and
mission.**
John Buchanan. Edinburgh: William Blackwood, 1885. 260p.
One of the first book-length accounts of early life in British Central Africa.
Buchanan went out as a missionary, but was dismissed following the 1881 Blantyre Mission scandal. Thereafter he became a prosperous businessman and served
as vice-consul. Two articles by the author are 'The industrial development of
Nyasaland', *Geographical Journal*, vol. 1 (1893), p. 245-53, and 'Journey along
the southern frontier of Nyassa-land', *Royal Geographic Society Proceedings*, vol.
17 (1891), p. 265-73.

3 **Cherries on my plate.**
Barbara Carr. Cape Town: Howard Timmins, 1965. 220p.
In 1940, after finishing school in England, the author took a ship to Beira, then
proceeded by train and automobile to Limbe and Zomba where she settled down
to run her father's household. He had been in the Protectorate for fifteen years,
first as a King's African Rifles officer, then as superintendent of the Central
Prison. The author describes her life in Nyasaland and South Africa and how she
met her future husband, a K.A.R. lieutenant who later became a game ranger.
Her married life is the subject of another volume entitled *Not for me the wilds*.

The Country and its People

4 Malawi's culture in the national integration.
Alifeyo Chilivumbo. *Présence Africaine*, vol. 22 (1976), p.
234-41.
A discussion of Malawi's cultural pluralism - its numerous ethnic groups, their
dances, music, drama and languages - and of how the independent government
has tried to bring about greater homogeneity through use of mass media. The
author points out that 'in the female dances, the movement and shaking of the
buttocks are particularly noticeable'.

5 Blantyre historical guide.
Paul A. Cole-King. Blantyre, Malawi: Christian Literature
Association in Malawi, 1973. 26p.
The writer was director of antiquities for several years after independence. This
interesting guide contains many old photographs of Blantyre and also advertise-
ments from early newspapers and government gazettes.

6 Lake Malawi steamers.
Paul A. Cole-King. Zomba, Malawi: Department of
Antiquities, 1971. 47p. (Historical Guides, no. 1).
This well-produced paperbound book features pictures and descriptions of vessels
which have operated on the lake and the Upper Shire River since 1900. It
includes the *Nkhwazi*, named after the fish eagles which are one of the most
familiar sights along the lakeshore.

7 Mangochi: the mountain, the people and the fort.
Paul A. Cole-King. Zomba, Malawi: Government Printer,
1972. 15p. (Department of Antiquities Publication, no. 12).
Located at the southern end of the lake, Mangochi - formerly Fort Johnston - has
been an area of considerable disquiet for the past century. First the Yao slave
raiders disrupted peoples' lives, then the colonial government had to suppress the
Yao. Finally, remoter parts of the region were used by post-independence dis-
sidents as launching points for several unsuccessful attempts to overthrow Dr.
Banda. The author also wrote *Cape Maclear*, (Department of Antiquities Publication, no. 4, 1968). Named by David Livingstone for the Royal Astronomer at
Cape Town, Cape Maclear is sixty miles north of Mangochi on the western
lakeshore.

8 My African neighbors: man, bird and beast in Nyasaland.
Hans Coudenhove. Boston, Massachusetts: Little, Brown,
1925. 245p.
The writer spent thirty years as a recluse in Tanganyika and Nyasaland, often
not seeing another European for months on end. His best friends were animals,
but he spent much time studying his African neighbours, especially the women,
who impressed him with their hard work, submissive nature and ability to keep
their babies quiet.

9 **Zomba Mountain: a walker's guide.**
H. M. Cundy, K. E. Cundy. Blantyre, Malawi: Malawi
Correspondence College, 1975. 33p.
'This guide is the result of many hours of enjoyable walking on Zomba Mountain.
Living on its bouldery slopes, we have had the privilege of knowing it in all
weathers and at all seasons, and the knowledge has been rewarding and restorat-
ive.' Included is a note on edible berries in the area.

10 **The hill of goodbye: the story of a solitary white woman's life
in Central Africa.**
Jessie Monteath Currie. London: Routledge, 1920. 249p.
This remarkable account describes life in Malawi during the 1890s. An artist who
did her own illustrations, the writer was interested in African medicine and also
wrote *With pole and paddle down the Shire and Zambesi.*

11 **African small chop.**
Sir Hector Duff. London: Hodder & Stoughton, 1932. 223p.
'Small chop' is West African slang for 'snack' or light informal meal. This
volume contains reminiscences of life in early Malawi and some material from
Yohani bin Abdullah on Yao customs. After serving as a civil servant, Duff
moved on to become governor of Tanganyika, then left Africa after the First
World War.

12 **Know your Rhodesia and know Nyasaland.**
Edited by N. S. Ferris. Salisbury: Rhodesian Printing &
Publishing Co., 1956. 316p.
A collection of 300 articles published from 1950 to 1956 in the *Rhodesian
Herald* newspaper as part of a series of the same name. Each of the short
selections is accompanied by a photograph. Those devoted to Malawi are few and
far between.

13 **Fourteen Africans vs. one American.**
Frederic Fox. New York: Macmillan, 1962. 171p.
Fox was a Congregational minister who worked in the White House for President
Eisenhower, then taught at the African Writing Centre in Kitwe, Zambia. 'Afri-
can number nine' was Malawian Bruce Wusikili who told the author he wanted
to become a journalist in order 'to promote faith, brotherhood, and leadership'.

14 **The story of Nyasaland.**
V. W. Hiller (and others). Salisbury: Central African
Archives, 1951. 95p.
Told in a series of historical pictures to commemorate the Diamond Jubilee of
Malawi, 1891-1951, this is a descriptive souvenir and catalogue of an exhibition
at the Salisbury Archives. It includes many details about Europeans and develop-
ment in the early days.

The Country and its People

15 **This Africa was mine.**
Emily Booth Langworthy. Stirling, Scotland: Stirling Tract
Enterprise, 1950. 139p.

This book describes the author's experience of arriving in British Central Africa as a ten-year-old in 1892 with her missionary father, Joseph Booth; their lives in a mud hut; John Chilembwe's nursing her through attacks of malaria; and other remarkable events, all recalled in great detail fifty years later. George Shepperson provided an introduction to this slim volume; the author was the grandmother of Dr. Harry Langworthy.

16 **Nyasaland for the hunter and settler.**
Denis D. Lyell. London: Horace Cox, 1912. 116p.

Lyell spent a considerable amount of time big-game hunting in Malawi at the turn of the century. He describes his adventures in this book, also in one called *The African elephant and its hunters* (London: Heath Cranton, 1924), and in another written with C. H. Stigand entitled *Central African game and its spoor.*

17 **Malawi.**
Pretoria: Africa Institute of South Africa, 1970. 36p. (Africa
at a Glance, no. 9).

The first eighteen pages of this short book give basic facts about Malawi in English for 1968-69 and include pictures. The second eighteen pages provide the same information in Afrikaans.

18 **Malawi.**
London: H.M. Stationery Office, 1964. 34p.

Part of a series of pamphlets produced by the British information services. Published to coincide with the granting of independence on 6 July 1964, it contains sections on the land and its people, economic and social progress, political progress, and some facts and figures which are out of date now but may be of interest to some readers.

19 **Malawi - the warm heart of Africa.**
Blantyre, Malawi: Mastward, 1978. 160p.

This guide for tourists and businessmen is the successor to the old colonial handbooks. It contains up-to-date information on customs, currency, communications, hunting, hotels, and places to visit, as well as descriptions of various regions of the country and the major companies operating there, plus colour photos and advertisements.

20 **Africa as I have known it: Nyasaland - East Africa - Liberia
- Senegal.**
R. C. F. Maugham. London: John Murray, 1929. 372p.
Reprinted, New York: Negro Universities Press.

When Maugham was a colonial administrator in Nyasaland he was known as R. C. Fulke-Greville, but he changed his name upon receiving an inheritance. This volume is full of colourful descriptions of life there during the 1890s and of some of the more eccentric characters who found their way to that remote corner of the world. 'Stores were full of the disagreeable odour of new calico, shelves were piled with mounds of cheap blankets, unattractive articles of delf and glassware, whitish opaline glass lamps, terribly thick tea-cups and tumblers unattractive to a degree.'.

21 Nyasaland in the nineties and other recollections.
R. C. F. Maugham. London: Lincoln Williams, 1935. 276p.
The purpose of this book was to describe 'the lighter and more amusing experiences of those who, during lengthy periods of their lives, have made the great Dark Continent their home'. The author also wrote *Wild game in Zambezia* (New York: Charles Scribner's Sons, 1914); and *Portuguese East Africa: the history, scenery and great game of Manica and Sofala* (1906). Maugham went on to become an important administrator and diplomat in West Africa.

22 Zambezi interlude.
Vivian Meik. London: Philip Allan, 1932. 245p.
A book of reminiscences; informally written by a person who worked in the railway section of the colonial administration.

23 American Universities Field Staff Reports. Central and Southern Africa Series.
Edwin S. Munger, James R. Hooker. Hanover, New Hampshire: American Universities Field Staff, 1969-71.
Professor Edwin S. Munger is a long-time student of African affairs, who taught in the geography departments of the University of Chicago and the California Institute of Technology, where the Munger Library is located. The late Dr. James R. Hooker was professor of African history at Michigan State University. With headquarters in Hanover, New Hampshire, the American Universities Field Staff (AUFS) represents a number of large American universities. Its associates are sent abroad to research and write journalistic articles on topics of current interest. Individual reports on Malawi written between 1969 and 1971 are situated under appropriate headings in this bibliography and in the index under their author's name.

24 The handbook of Nyasaland.
S. S. Murray. London: Crown Agents for the Colonies, for the Government of Nyasaland, 1932. 4th ed. 436p.
A general, descriptive and economic guide to the country, issued first in 1908 during Sir Alfred Sharpe's governorship, with later editions in 1910 and 1922. These are very useful books for the curious, containing information on everything from the best treatment for dysentery - Epsom salts four to six times daily - to the fact that the excrement of civet cats can always be identified by the large number of wild fruit seeds found in it.

25 Area handbook for Malawi.
Harold D. Nelson (and others). Washington, D.C.: U.S. Government Printing Office, 1975. xiv+353p. (DA Pam 550-172).
Prepared at the request of the U.S. Army, by Foreign Area Studies (FAS) of the American University, Washington, D.C., this is part of a series of handbooks covering every country in the world. It includes basic information on all aspects of Malawian life.

The Country and its People

26 Ten Africans.
Dame Margery Perham. London: Faber, 1936. 356p. map.

Each chapter in this book is a mini-biography of a 'typical African'. Chapter 6 is 'The story of Amini bin Saidi of the Yao tribe of Nyasaland' as recorded by D. W. Malcolm. Amini worked in Tanganyika for many years, mostly as a house servant, but still preferred his lakeside home. 'Nyasaland is a better country than Tanganyika. I only stay in Tanganyika because the pay is better.' This was a universal attitude among Malawians, who emigrated to neighbouring countries in large numbers searching for jobs during the colonial period.

27 A portrait of Malawi.
Zomba, Malawi: Government Printer, 1964. 119p.

This paperbound volume was published on the occasion of Malawi's independence. The text is divided into three parts: the past, the land, and the people; it is supplemented by black and white photos, illustrations and drawings from early works on the country.

28 Mandala trail: a tale of early days in Nyasaland.
Wilfrid Robertson. London, New York: Oxford University Press, 1956. 184p.

A fictionalized account of Nyasaland during the 1880s and 1890s, centring on the development of the African Lakes Company, the Moir brothers and their battle with Mlozi.

29 The cook book.
Annabel Shaxson, Pat Dixon, June Walker. Zomba, Malawi: Government Printer, 1974. 173p.

This popular Malawi cookbook was compiled to provide interesting recipes for all races. In their introduction the authors 'hope that it will encourage housewives to be more adventurous in their cooking and to use the large variety of fruits and vegetables available in the country'. A recipe for two persons for *nsima* - the thick, maize-meal porridge which is the staple food for most of the population - calls for 1 cup *ufa* (maize flour), 3 cups water, and butter or margarine. *Ufa* and lukewarm water are stirred together, brought to a boil and stirred until well cooked. Butter or margarine is added and the dish is served with meat, fish or vegetables. Also see *Nyasaland cookery book and household guide* (Blantyre: Nyasaland Council of Women, 1947).

30 Smiling Malawi.
Zomba, Malawi: for the Malawi Government, 1976. 143p.

A beautifully produced tenth anniversary publication, sponsored by the Malawi government, which contains a 20-page introduction describing the country and its background and 100 pages of photographs. An extra bonus is 'The voice of Ngwazi Kamuzu Banda', a long-playing record of speeches, the national anthem, and other songs.

The Country and its People

31 Green gold: from South-East Asia to Central Africa - a story of a tea estate in Malawi.
Arthur Westrop. Bulawayo, Rhodesia: Cauldwell Cards [n.d.]. 491p.

The last governor-general of Malawi, Sir Glyn Jones, wrote an introduction to this fascinating autobiography. It is dedicated to 'all drinkers of tea, particularly the British housewife'. Before settling at Magombe Estate in Thyolo, the author grew tea in Malaya, India and Ceylon and was interned in a Japanese P.O.W. camp. For more about 'green gold' see *Tea in Malawi*, published for The Tea Association (Central Africa) Ltd. by the University Press of Africa (1968).

32 Malawi: profile of an in-between country.
Eric Lloyd Williams. *Optima*, vol. 22, pt. 3 (Sept. 1972), p. 110-29.

The author is a public relations manager for Anglo-American Corporation in Johannesburg and a former Washington correspondent for the South African Press Association. This article presents a general description of economic development projects, especially in the new capital of Lilongwe.

33 Legumes in the diet of the Nyasaland African.
Jessie Williamson. *Nyasaland Journal*, vol. 7, pt. 1 (Jan. 1954), p. 19-29.

A useful article by a nutritionist on Malawian diet. *Nsima* usually goes along with a flavoured and salted cooked dish called *ndiwo*, consisting of leaves with groundnuts, vegetables or meat. For more on raising food in Malawi see the Lilongwe Agricultural Society's *Garden note book* (Blantyre: Blantyre Print [n.d.]).

34 Year book and guide of the Rhodesias and Nyasaland, with biographies.
Salisbury: Rhodesian Publications, 1937-?

Publication has now ceased. Covered all aspects of the countries and their life, although relatively few of the pages related to Nyasaland.

Early Blantyre.
See item no. 177.

7

Geography

35 **The waters of Malawi: developments since independence, 1966-1976.**
Swanzie Agnew. Zomba, Malawi: Chancellor College [1976]. 49p. (Department of Geography and Earth Sciences. Occasional Paper, no. 1).
A historical study of Malawi's water resources.

36 **Malawi in maps.**
Edited by Swanzie Agnew, G. Michael Stubbs. London: University of London Press; New York: Holmes & Meier, 1972. 143p. bibliog.
An excellent geography of Malawi which presents - for the first time - demographic, economic, social, and population information in map form. Including a select bibliography and statistical appendices, it amounts to a national atlas. The editors had full government co-operation in compiling their materials. Two Malawians, J. Lupoka and B. Makwiti, drew the maps. For more by Swanzie Agnew, formerly professor of geography and earth sciences at the University of Malawi, see 'Environment and history: the Malawian setting', in *Malawi: the history of a nation* (q.v.), edited by Bridglal Pachai, p. 28-48.

37 **Geomorphology and the Mlanje Mountain.**
Colin A. Baker. *Society of Malawi Journal*, vol. 19, pt. 1 (Jan. 1966), p. 21-31.
The author discusses erosion and its effects on shaping Mount Mulanje. The oldest rocks in the area are from the pre-Cambrian period, 500 million years ago.

38 **The geology and geomorphology of Zomba Mountain.**
K. Bloomfield, Anthony Young. *Nyasaland Journal*, vol. 14, pt. 2 (July 1961), p. 54-80.
Fine views can be seen from the top of Zomba Mountain: to the west the Kirk Range, to the east Lake Chilwa, and to the southeast Mount Mulanje.

39 The geography of N'yassi.
W. D. Cooley. *Journal of the Royal Geographical Society*, vol. 15 (1845), p. 185-235.

This article, although containing the mistaken hypothesis that one large lake existed instead of Lakes Malawi and Tanganyika, presents valuable information gathered from men with first-hand experience of the area. It contains testimonies from the Omani Arab, Khamis bin Uthman; his Yao slave, Nasib; and an Arab merchant, Mohammed bin Nassur, and important facts about Yao country. Helpful in sorting out facts from fancy is Roy Bridges's article, 'W. D. Cooley, the R.G.S. and African geography in the nineteenth century', *Geographical Journal*, vol. 142, pt. 1 (March 1976), p. 27-47, and vol. 142, pt. 2 (July 1976), p. 274-86.

40 Zomba flood, December, 1946.
A. C. Talbot Edwards. *Nyasaland Journal*, vol. 1, pt. 2 (July 1948), p. 53-63.

During this exceptional storm twenty-six inches of rain fell in under forty hours causing serious landslides on Zomba Mountain which damaged houses and government buildings, tore up roads, and killed twenty-one Africans in two villages.

41 Northern Nyasaland.
James Henderson. *Scottish Geographical Magazine*, vol. 16 (1900), p. 82-9.

The Revd. Henderson collected his information on trips through the region between 1895 and 1899. He describes the country as 'exceptionally wild and rugged' and divided into three belts, each running parallel to the lake: the coast and its plain, the first or Tumbuka plateau, and the second or Nyika plateau. For another early description of the area see Richard Crawshay, 'A journey in the Angoni country', *Geographical Journal*, vol. 3 (1897), p. 59-60. In 1893, Crawshay was the first government agent stationed at Deep Bay, now Chirumba.

42 A note on the underground water resources of the Protectorate.
D. N. Holt. *Nyasaland Journal*, vol. 12, pt. 2 (July 1959), p. 60-82.

From 1923, a systematic programme of well digging and water-hole boring was carried out, and by 1956, 729 boreholes and 456 wells had been sunk in Malawi. This paper discusses the water-finding methods of divining, geophysical surveying, and surface observation, and provides information on underground water supplies by geographical region - for the Rift Valley, the scarps and foothills, and the highland plateaus.

43 Malawi's new capital city: a regional planning perspective.
J. Ngoleka Mlia. *Pan-African Journal*, vol. 8, pt. 4 (1975), p. 387-402.

Dr. Mlia teaches in the Department of Geography and Earth Sciences of the University of Malawi. His paper adopts a regional development and planning perspective in its discussion of the Malawi government's decision to build a new capital at Lilongwe, in spite of the high opportunity costs involved. Also see J.

Geography

Connell, 'Lilongwe: another new capital for Africa', in *East African Geographical Review*, no. 10 (1 April 1972).

44 Malawi: a geographical study.
John G. Pike, G. T. Rimmington. London, New York: Oxford University Press, 1965. 229p.

This work is in two parts; the first, by Pike, is on physical geography - geology, climate and weather, soils and vegetation; the second, by Rimmington, is on historical, social and economic geography, including rural settlement patterns, major crops, export trade, natural resources and their development.

45 The hydrology of Lake Malawi.
John G. Pike. *Society of Malawi Journal*, vol. 21, pt. 2 (July 1968), p. 20-47.

This paper deals with the geology, physiography, climate, vegetation, soils and hydrology of the lake, with a view to providing an estimate of the various portions of the water balance. Run-off over the land is shown to be increasing, making stabilization and regulation more difficult.

46 The sunspot/lake level relationship and the control of Lake Malawi.
John G. Pike. *Society of Malawi Journal*, vol. 21, pt. 2 (July 1968), p. 48-59.

This article disputes the sunspot/free water analogy used to predict lake levels. An early proponent of this theory was F. Dixey in 'Lake level in relation to rainfall and sunspots', *Nature*, vol. 114 (1924), p. 659.

47 The historical geography of population growth in the Dedza District of Nyasaland.
Gerald T. Rimmington. *Nyasaland Journal*, vol. 16, pt. 2 (July 1963), p. 43-60.

The author comments on the agro-economic problems arising from scarcity of land, and on the increasing markets for cash crops, both of which have resulted from the rapid growth of the African and Asian population in the Dedza District. He predicts the numbers of European mission and administrative workers will decline as Africanization of their posts continues, and notes that the number of white planters in the district is negligible. Rimmington published a companion study, 'Village types in the Kachindamoto area of the Dedza District of Nyasaland', in *Nyasaland Journal*, vol. 17, pt. 1 (Jan. 1964), p. 7-9.

48 A map of the distribution of major biotic communities in Malawi.
T. F. Shaxson. *Society of Malawi Journal*, vol. 30, pt. 1 (Jan. 1977), p. 35-48.

Part of a wider study of Southern Africa undertaken by the Southern African Regional Commission for the Conservation and Utilization of the Soil (SARC-CUS). For more on this topic, see J. D. Chapman, 'The conservation of vegetation and its individual species in Malawi', in *Acta Phytogeographica Suecica*, vol. 54 (1966), p. 215-24.

49 Note on the surface water resources of the Protectorate.

G. A. N. Starmans. *Nyasaland Journal*, vol. 10, pt. 1 (Jan. 1957), p. 24-44.

This article contains a hydrological analysis of the country; discussions of the drainage areas of each of the three regions; sections on evaporation, soil loss, dams and floods; and closes with several pages on the possibilities for increasing useful surface water supplies. The author calls for the protection and covering of watersheds, the control of river banks and for detailed soil conservation measures. Another paper on the same subject is E. W. Latham, 'Water resources and water development in Nyasaland', *Nyasaland Journal*, vol. 17, no. 2 (July 1964), p. 57-70.

50 Survey of the eastern coast of Lake Nyassa and latest news of the 'Lake-Junction Road'.

James Stewart, C.E. *Proceedings of the Royal Geographical Society*, vol. 12 (Dec. 1883), p. 689-92.

James Stewart, C.E., should not be confused with his contemporary, Dr. James Stewart, who wrote on the same subject. The 'Lake-Junction Road' refers to the Stevenson Road linking Lakes Nyasa and Tanganyika. The article contains a letter of 2 July 1883 from Stewart to James Stevenson, written a month before the death of the author.

51 The second circumnavigation of Lake Nyassa.

Dr. James Stewart. *Proceedings of the Royal Geographical Society*, vol. 5 (May 1879), p. 289-304.

E. D. Young was the first to reach the north end of the lake (see his *Nyassa: a journal of adventures*, and *The search for Livingstone* elsewhere in this bibliography). This event took place on the lake steamer *Ilala* in Sept. 1877. Also on board was H. B. Cotterill who recorded his impressions in an article called 'The Nyassa with notes on the slave trade, and the prospects of commerce and colonization of that region', in the *Journal of the Society of Arts* (7 June 1878), p. 678-83. For a more recent report see R. A. Kemp, *A voyage round Lake Nyasa* (Likoma Island, Malawi: Universities' Mission Press [n.d.]).

52 The geology of the Mchinji - Upper Bua area.

E. C. Thatcher, K. E. Wilderspin. Zomba, Malawi: Government Printer, 1968. 72p. (Geological Survey of Malawi, Bulletin 24).

The Geological Survey Department of the Ministry of Natural Resources has tried unsuccessfully to discover valuable minerals in Malawi. Among other publications on the subject are: Malawi Ministry of Economic Affairs, *Records of the Geological Survey of Malawi* (Zomba: Government Printer, 1959-65), 7 vols.; E. C. Thatcher, *The geology of the Dedza area* (Zomba: Government Printer, 1968); W. G. G. Cooper and F. Habgood, *The geology of the Livingstonia Coalfield* (Zomba: Government Printer, 1959); E. C. Thatcher and M. J. Walter, *The geology of the South Lilongwe Plain and Dzalanyama Range* (Zomba: Government Printer, 1968); K. Bloomfield, *Infracrustal ring-complexes of Southern Malawi* (Zomba: Government Printer, 1965); K. Bloomfield, *The pre-Karroo geology of Malawi* (Zomba: Government Printer, 1968); R. Keith Evans, *The geology of the Shire Highlands* (Zomba: Government Printer, 1965); A. L. Dawson, *The geology of the Lake Chiuta area* (Zomba: Government Printer, 1970); E. R. Peters, *The geology of the Kasungu area* (Zomba: Government

Geography

Printer, 1969); and D. N. Holt, *The Kangankunde Hill rare earth prospect* (Zomba: Government Printer, 1965).

53 A geography of Malawi.

Anthony Young, Doreen M. Young. London: Dent, 1964. 72p. New ed., London: Evans Brothers, 1974.

A schools' geography textbook published to coincide with independence. Many of the place-names and spellings have since changed, rendering it out of date.

54 Memories of the Nyika Plateau.

W. P. Young. *Nyasaland Journal*, vol. 6, pt. 1 (Jan. 1953), p. 45-52.

These memoirs of a 1913 visit to the plateau were prompted by Laurens van der Post's book (*Venture to the interior* (q.v.)). Young's article in turn elicited three more short contributions in *Nyasaland Journal*, vol. 7, pt. 2 (July 1954): 'The Nyika Plateau by Richard Crawshay's impression in 1893', p. 24-7; 'C. W. Benson's visits, 1937-53', p. 28-34; and L. J. Brass, 'Vernay Expedition report, 1946', p. 35-8. Other Nyika articles include R. G. M. Willan, 'A visit to the Nyika in 1937', *Nyasaland Journal*, vol. 9, pt. 2 (July 1956), p. 51-6; Margaret Stewart, 'On top of Malawi - the Misuku', *Nyasaland Journal*, vol. 18, pt. 1 (Jan. 1965), p. 7-13; two by Mrs. Stewart's husband, Paul Lemon: 'The Nyika wildlife frontier', *Nyasaland Journal*, vol. 17, pt. 2 (July 1964), p. 29-41, and 'Biology of zebra on Nyika Plateau', *Society of Malawi Journal*, vol. 21, pt. 1 (Jan. 1968), p. 13-19; and C. W. Benson, 'Nyasaland and Northern Rhodesia: the Nyika Plateau and its faunistic significance', *Oryx*, pt. 2 (1953).

Nyasaland, the land of the lake.
See item no. 109.

The physical environment of Northern Nyasaland with special reference to soils and agriculture.
See item no. 467.

Flora and Fauna

55 **An alleged record of the chimpanzee Pan Satyrus in Malawi.**
C. W. Benson. *Society of Malawi Journal*, vol. 21, pt. 1
(Jan. 1968), p. 7-12.

This article terminated a controversy which raged for years among a very small group of people about whether or not there was a female chimpanzee living around Nkhata Bay in 1959. Benson, a former district commissioner at Chinteche, argues convincingly that there was no natural chimpanzee population in Northern Malawi. The lone individual sighted by a number of people was an escapee from a travelling circus. See also B. L. Mitchell and C. S. Holliday, 'A new primate from Nyasaland', *South African Journal of Science*, vol. 59 (1960), p. 215-22; R. G. M. Willan, 'Ufiti - Nyasaland's "mystery" animal - is an ordinary chimp', *Wild Life* (Nairobi), vol. 3 (1961), p. 21-4; and W. C. Osman Hill, 'Ufiti: the present position', *Symposia of the Zoological Society of London*, no. 10 (1963), p. 57-9.

56 **The bird-life of Lake Nyasa.**
C. W. Benson. *Nyasaland Journal*, vol. 4, pt. 2 (July 1951),
p. 49-66.

In contrast to the fish of Lake Malawi, there are no bird species peculiar to it. This paper lists birds observed by the author at the lake and gives previously unpublished impressions of the call of Pel's fishing owl and of the breeding call and 'drumming' of the Ethiopian snipe. It also records an observation of the tufted duck, previously unknown south of Northern Tanzania. Information is provided on breeding, but the author confesses ignorance about the significance of the lake, and the Rift Valley as a whole, as a migratory route. For years Benson was a prolific writer on Malawi's birdlife and published many articles not listed in this volume, especially in the journal *Ibis*. For more on birds see Sir Charles Belcher, *Birds of Nyasaland* (1930); G. G. M. Schulten and G. B. Harrison, 'An annotated list of birds recorded at Lake Chilwa', *Society of Malawi Journal*, vol. 28, pt. 2 (July 1975), p. 6-30; and R. W. Borden, M. J. Roberts, D. J. Allen, R. C. Coffin and M. Mannion, 'Birds of Bunda', *Society of Malawi Journal*, vol. 28, pt. 1, (Jan. 1975), p. 54-72.

Flora and Fauna

57 A first check list of the herbaceous flora of Malawi.
Blodwen Binns. Zomba, Malawi: Government Printer, 1968.
113p.

A book by the professor of botany at the University of Malawi. Also see: J. Burtt Davy, A. C. Hoyle and P. Topham, *Check list of the forest trees and shrubs of the Nyasaland Protectorate* (Zomba: Government Printer, 1958), and R. G. Jackson and P. Wiehe, *An annotated check list of Nyasaland grasses* (Zomba: Government Printer, 1958). The definitive flora of the region is *Flora Zambesiaca*, edited by A. W. Excell, H. Wild, J. P. M. Brenan, and A. Fernandes (London: Crown Agents for Overseas Governments and Administrations, 1961-70), 3 vols., which covers Malawi, Zambia, Rhodesia, Mozambique and Botswana.

58 Dictionary of plant names in Malawi.
Blodwen Binns. Zomba, Malawi: Government Printer, 1972.
184p.

As the author points out in her introduction, 'This dictionary has been prepared with the two-fold aim of presenting in a compact form a directory of the scientific names of most of the genera of plants in Malawi, and of the vernacular names of many of their species'. The section on vernacular names was edited by J. P. Logah, senior education officer, Ministry of Education.

59 Ethnobotany of plant names in Malawi: their origins and meanings.
Blodwen Binns. *Society of Malawi Journal*, vol. 29, pt. 1 (Jan. 1976), p. 46-57.

A useful article for cultural historians as well as for botanists. African names are given for both indigenous and introduced plants. For the latter, information is provided on the ways and means of their introduction into Malawi.

60 Vegetation of Nyasaland: report on the Vernay Nyasaland Expedition of 1946.
L. J. Brass. *Memoirs of the New York Botanical Garden*, vol. 8, pt. 3 (June 1953).

This expedition, sponsored by the American Museum of Natural History, was led by Arthur S. Vernay, a trustee of the museum, and included Harold E. Anthony of the museum; Captain Guy Shortridge of the Kaffrarian Museum, King William's Town, South Africa; and Brass, who represented the New York Botanical Garden. Its purpose was to collect mammals, fish, reptiles, amphibians, insects and plants, of which 2,004 were numbered. Also see: J. P. M. Brenan and collaborators, 'Plants collected by the Vernay Expedition of 1946', *Memoirs of the New York Botanical Garden*, vol. 8, pt. 3 (June 1953); Harold E. Anthony, 'A succulent enthusiast in Nyasaland', *Journal of the New York Botanical Garden*, vol. 50 (1949), p. 17-30; L. J. Brass, 'Plant hunting in Nyasaland and botanical notes on some other parts of Africa', *Journal of the New York Botanical Garden*, vol. 49 (1948), p. 105-19, 129-37; James Britten (et al.), 'The plants of Milanji, Nyasa-land', *Transactions of the Linnean Society of London. Botany*, 2nd series, vol. 4 (1894), p. 1-67; R. G. M. Willan, 'Notes on the vegetation of northern Nyasaland', *Empire Forestry Journal*, no. 19 (1940), p. 48-61; and F. Dixey, 'The Mlanje Mountains of Nyasaland', *Geographical Review*, vol. 17 (1927), p. 611-26.

61 Some notes on the taxonomy, distribution, ecology and economic importance of Widdringtonia, with particular reference to W. Whytei.

J. D. Chapman. *Nyasaland Journal*, vol. 13, pt. 1 (Jan. 1960), p. 65-86.

Widdringtonias are known as the 'African cypresses'. W. Whytei is called the 'Mulanje cedar'. It is a remarkably durable wood, completely insect-proof, but not useful for boxes or cabinets because of its high resin content. It is found on Mulanje and Mchese Mountains and is used in Malawi as common building timber and for making furniture.

62 The vegetation of the Mlanje Mountains, Nyasaland: a preliminary account with particular reference to the Widdringtonia forests.

J. D. Chapman. Zomba, Malawi: Government Printer, 1962. 78p. 25 plates.

Mulanje is an isolated massif, of nearly 200 square miles, whose sides rise abruptly from the surrounding plains. Nearly the whole of the range is included within the Mulanje Mountains Forest Reserve, under control of the Forestry Department.

63 The evergreen forests of Malawi.

J. D. Chapman, F. White. Oxford, England: University of Oxford, Commonwealth Forestry Institute, 1970. 190p.

The evergreen forests of Malawi are not extensive and produce little timber, but they are important in preventing soil erosion and flooding and in maintaining water supplies. Chapman collected nearly 3,000 specimens of evergreen during his thirteen years of service with the colonial Forestry Department. White's knowledge covers a large area of African forest flora. A recurrent theme in the book is the interdependence of ecology, phytogeography and taxonomy. Another article on this subject is by R. G. M. Willan, 'Indigenous trees of Nyasaland', *Nyasaland Journal*, vol. 12, pt. 1 (Jan. 1959), p. 50-6.

64 Chromosomes in cultivated crops.

B. B. Chimphamba. Zomba, Malawi: University of Malawi Research and Publications Committee, 1978. 79p.

The author is the dean of the School of Science in the University of Malawi and the principal of Chancellor College. He is also a biologist specializing in cytogenetics, and this book is his University of London Ph.d. thesis, 'intended as a short account of chromosome manipulation' in plants common to Malawi.

65 Succulents of Chitipa - the muddy place.

Bruce J. Hargreaves. *Society of Malawi Journal*, vol. 30, pt. 1 (Jan. 1977), p. 28-35.

Chitipa means 'muddy place'. It is one of the northernmost towns in Malawi and has an average annual rainfall of thirty-five to forty inches. Succulents are plants adapted to arid conditions, but they may occur - as in this case - in the arid niches of areas which receive normal rainfall. See also G. W. Reynolds, *The aloes of Nyasaland* (Blantyre: Nyasaland Society, 1954).

Flora and Fauna

66 **Wildlife conservation in Malawi.**
G. D. Hayes. *Society of Malawi Journal*, vol. 25, pt. 2
(July 1972), p. 22-31.

Hayes was the long-time vice-chairman of the Society of Malawi until 1973 when, upon the death of the society's first chairman, Sir Malcolm Barrow, he assumed the post. This article describes Malawi's game parks.

67 **A guide to Malawi's national parks and game reserves.**
G. D. Hayes. Zomba, Malawi: Government Printer [1972].
xi + 118p.

A very comprehensive guide to Malawi's game parks, which includes a note on conservation, plus descriptions of the various animals to be found in the country and how to track them. Also see G. D. Hayes, 'Conservation in Malawi - old and new', *Oryx*, vol. 12, pt. 3.

68 **The dry woodlands of Nyasaland.**
Charles R. Hursh. Salisbury: International Co-operation
Administration, 1960. 47p.

This report is divided into two parts: the first deals with general forestry problems and their significance; desirable timber species in woodland associations, the nature and origin of the brachystegia woodlands, and the composition of the dry woodlands; the second deals with the silviculture and management of the dry woodlands, regeneration studies, and forest research possibilities. The author was associated with the U.S. Forest Service.

69 **The grasslands of Malawi, parts I and II.**
George Jackson. *Society of Malawi Journal*, vol. 22, pt. 1
(Jan. 1969), p. 7-25; vol. 22, pt. 2 (July 1969), p. 73-82.

The author argues that the montane grasslands of Malawi are not edaphic, as suggested by an earlier writer, but developed from montane forest. The swamp grasslands are edaphic, as waterlogging excludes the growth of trees. Evergreen forests have no grasslands, but deciduous woodlands do. See also George Jackson, 'The vegetation of Malawi', *Society of Malawi Journal*, vol. 21, pt. 2 (July 1968), p. 11-19; and George Jackson and P. O. Wiehe, *An annotated check list of Nyasaland grasses, indigenous and cultivated* (Zomba: Government Printer, 1958).

70 *Mbuna* - **rock dwelling cichlids of Lake Malawi, Africa.**
P. B. N. Jackson, Tony Ribbinck. Neptune City, New
Jersey; Reigate, England: T. F. H. Publications, 1975. 128p.

This book about small fish in Lake Malawi is full of beautiful colour photographs. The authors are associated with the J. L. B. Smith Institute of Ichthyology at Rhodes University in Grahamstown, South Africa, and spent two years researching their subject at Nkhata Bay.

71 **The fishes of Lake Chilwa.**
R. G. Kirk. *Society of Malawi Journal*, vol. 20, pt. 1 (Jan. 1967), p. 35-48.

Lake Chilwa is the twelfth largest lake in Africa, with an open water area of 260 square miles. There is no evidence of any previous connection with Lake Malawi. Probably Lakes Chilwa and Chiuta were formerly one, and drained into the Ruo River, then into the Shire. Twelve species of fish occur in the lake's saline waters, but only three are numerous enough to be of economic importance. A companion article in the same issue is A. J. P. Mzumara, 'The Lake Chilwa fisheries', p. 58-68.

72 **Our enemy the crocodile.**
Freda Klamborowski. *Nyasaland Journal*, vol. 17, pt. 2 (July 1964), p. 51-6.

An original member of the Nyasaland Society, Klamborowski spent over fifty years as an Anglican missionary teacher at Likoma Island, Mponda's and Malindi. She was awarded an M.B.E., and died in 1971 in Blantyre at the age of eighty-seven. Her article recounts the fatalities caused by crocodiles which she witnessed over the years. See 'Miss Frederica May Klamborowski', *Society of Malawi Journal*, vol. 24, pt. 2 (July 1971), p. 80-2.

73 **Aquatic birds of Blantyre.**
H. T. Laycock. *Nyasaland Journal*, vol. 13, pt. 1 (Jan. 1960), p. 7-17.

New reservoirs in the area attracted many new species of aquatic birds: grebes, egrets, cormorants, ducks, fish eagles, geese, sandpipers, plovers, kingfishers and coots. Also see: H. T. Laycock, 'Aquatic birds of Blantyre', *Nyasaland Journal*, vol. 19, pt. 1 (Jan. 1966), p. 49-64; F. E. White, 'The birds of an African garden', *Nyasaland Journal*, vol. 13, pt. 2 (July 1960), p. 22-34; and G. B. Harrison, 'Aquatic birds at a dam at Chileka', *Nyasaland Journal*, vol. 17, pt. 2 (July 1964), p. 42-50.

74 **A list with notes of the mammals of the Nsanje - Port Herald - District Malawi.**
R. Charles Long. *Society of Malawi Journal*, vol. 26, pt. 1 (Jan. 1973), p. 60-78.

Among the mammals listed by the Revd. Long are the short-snouted elephant shrew; the giant musk shrew; the Egyptian slit-faced bat; the thick tailed galago, commonly called a bush baby; the zorilla, a beast combining the worst characteristics of the weasel, badger and skunk; and the African giant rat which grows to three feet in length with an eighteen-inch tail. See also: P. Hanney and B. Morris, 'Some observations upon the pouched rat in Nyasaland', *Journal of Mammalogy*, vol. 43, pt. 2 (1962), p. 238-48; W. D. S. Talbot, 'A few notes on hippopotamus hunting by the Phodzo people of Port Herald District using harpoons', *Nyasaland Journal*, vol. 9, pt. 2 (1956); and D. W. K. Macpherson, 'Wild life of the central regions', *Society of Malawi Journal*, vol. 26, pt. 2 (July 1973), p. 48-55, a reminiscence of the author's experiences with wildlife in the late 1920s.

Flora and Fauna

75 **The birds of Nsanje - Port Herald - District.**
R. Charles Long. *Society of Malawi Journal*, vol. 26, pt. 2 (July 1973), p. 56-79; vol. 27, pt. 1 (Jan. 1974), p. 74-88; vol. 29, pt. 1 (Jan. 1976), p. 6-34; *Ostrich* (1960), p. 85-104; (1961), p. 23-35, 147-73.

The Revd. Long began keeping detailed daily records of birds observed in Southern Malawi in 1951. See also R. J. Dowsett, 'Some new bird distribution records of Malawi', *Society of Malawi Journal*, vol. 27, pt. 2 (July 1974), p. 32-6.

76 **The breeding colonies of large water and marsh birds within the Port Herald District.**
R. Charles Long. *Nyasaland Journal*, vol. 9, pt. 2 (July 1956), p. 29-50.

Discusses the distribution and breeding habits of cormorants, pelicans, herons and storks in Southern Malawi.

77 **Notes on the ecology of Lake Nyasa fish.**
Rosemary H. Lowe. *Nyasaland Journal*, vol. 1, pt. 1 (Jan. 1948), p. 39-50.

Between 1945 and 1947, the author conducted a survey of fish in the lake, and recorded thirteen different families. Of the 223 species she found, eighty per cent belonged to the Cichlidae family. Isolated by the falls on the Shire River, many new species developed in the lake; eighty-seven per cent of them are found nowhere else in the world. The *chambo* (*Tilapia squamipinnis*), a relative of the perch, is one of the commonest of all lake fish and makes a delicious meal. See also Peter R. Morgan, 'The culture of Tilapia Shirana Chilwae in fish-ponds', *Society of Malawi Journal*, vol. 24, pt. 2 (July 1971), p. 74-9.

78 **Growth and silviculture of *Pinus patula* in Malawi.**
H. G. W. Marshall, D. L. Foot. Zomba, Malawi: Government Printer, 1969. 58p.

Pinus patula is the most important plantation tree in Malawi.

79 **Game preservation in Nyasaland.**
B. L. Mitchell. *Nyasaland Journal*, vol. 6, pt. 2 (July 1953), p. 37-51.

In 1897, Sir Alfred Sharpe established the country's first game preserve at Elephant Marsh, along the southern reaches of the Shire River. Thereafter, additional preserves and non-shooting areas came into· being near Nkhotakota, Kasungu, on the Nyika Plateau and in Southern Region. This article describes the flora and fauna of these places.

80 **Wild flowers of Malawi.**
Audrey Moriarty. Johannesburg, South Africa: Purnell, 1975. 166p.

A lovely book with painted illustrations by the author.

81 Epiphytic orchids of the Limbuli stream, Mlanje.

Brian Morris. *Society of Malawi Journal*, vol. 18, pt. 2 (July 1965), p. 59-70.

Limbuli stream is a tributary of the Malosa River, and epiphytic orchids are those which grow on trees rather than on the ground. Nine species of epiphytics belonging to eight genera were found on Mulanje in gallery forest between 3,000 and 4,000 feet above sea level. Over fifty species of this kind of orchid have been recorded in the Shire Highlands. The author also contributed 'The epiphytic orchids of Soche Mountain', *Society of Malawi Journal*, vol. 20, pt. 2 (July 1967), p. 30-9.

82 The mammals of Rhodesia, Zambia and Malawi.

Reay H. N. Smithers. London: Collins, 1966. 159p.

The author was director of the National Museums of Rhodesia. This volume contains descriptions of ninety-six species visitors are likely to see; details of their habitat, breeding, diet and other habits; eighty reproductions of tracks; and sixty distribution maps. Illustrations of the animals were done by the American artist, E. J. Bierly. Also see Brian Morris, 'Mammals of Zoa Estate Cholo', *Nyasaland Journal*, vol. 17, pt. 2 (July 1964), p. 71-8; W. F. H. Ansell, C. W. Benson and B. L. Mitchell, 'Notes on some mammals of Nyasaland and adjacent areas', *Nyasaland Journal*, vol. 16, pt. 1 (Jan. 1962), p. 38-54.

83 Amphibians of Malawi.

Margaret M. Stewart. Albany, New York: State University of New York Press, 1967. 163p.

This book is illustrated by the author and dedicated to the children of Malawi. The first amphibian collections in the country were made in the 1890s by Alexander Whyte, Harry Johnston's naturalist. Since then many biologists have studied the sixty species of amphibians and have been delighted by the multicoloured fantastically patterned frogs of Central Africa.

84 Relation of fire to habitat preference of small animals on the Nyika Plateau, Malawi.

Margaret M. Stewart. *Society of Malawi Journal*, vol. 25, pt. 1 (Jan. 1972), p. 33-42.

'Habitats preferred by small mammals on the Nyika Plateau, Malawi, are rank cover of bracken - sedge - weeds, pine plantations, and boggy grassland with dense cover. Few animals occurred on unburned grassland far from water. Grassland areas subject to annual burning yielded more small mammals than did unburned grasslands.' Also see J. C. Cater, 'The Nyika Plateau, Nyasaland', in *Oryx*, pt. 2 (1954); P. Hanney, 'The harsh-furred rat in Nyasaland', *Journal of Mammalogy*, vol. 45 (1964).

85 Snakes of Nyasaland.

R. C. H. Sweeney. Zomba, Malawi: Government Printer, 1961. 200p.

Of forty-eight different species of snakes identified in Nyasaland, fourteen are dangerous, but only five of these are common and then only in restricted localities. This volume could have used more illustrations. Also see A. Loveridge, 'Zoological results of a fifth expedition to East Africa, III: reptiles from Nyasal-

Flora and Fauna

and and Tete', *Bulletin of the Museum of Comparative Zoology*, no. 110 (1953), p. 143-322.

86 The Chelonia of Nyasaland Protectorate.
R. C. H. Sweeney. *Nyasaland Journal*, vol. 13, pt. 1 (Jan. 1960), p. 35-50.
Chelonia are tortoises and terrapins; there are six species in the country: the hinged tortoise, the eastern leopard tortoise, the mud turtle, the Cape terrapin, the black terrapin and the serrated terrapin. Sweeney is also author of *A check list of the mammals of Nyasaland*, published by the Nyasaland Society.

87 Nyasaland trees and shrubs.
Paul Topham. *Nyasaland Journal*, vol. 5, pt. 2 (July 1952), p. 11-17.
Mentions a few of the bewildering number of species in the country. Over 1,000 different kinds of trees have been collected within fifty miles of Limbe alone. For a list of their diseases see W. T. H. Peregrine and M. A. Siddiqi, *A revised and annotated list of plant diseases in Malawi* (Kew, England: Commonwealth Mycological Institute, 1972. (Phytopathological Papers, no. 16)).

88 Preliminary list of some edible fungi.
Jessie Williamson. *Society of Malawi Journal*, vol. 26, pt. 1 (Jan. 1973), p. 15-27.
The author claims that knowledge of edible fungi is dying out as young girls attend school instead of going into the bush with older women to gather foods. The edible fungi include the common mushroom, various gill fungi, and pore fungi. The author, a nutritionist with thirty years' experience of Malawian diet, states that the common belief that Malawians are protein-starved is a myth because their diet of maize supplemented with beans, peas and groundnuts provides all the amino acids required by a normal person. Also see, by the same author, 'Some edible fungi of Malawi', *Society of Malawi Journal*, vol. 27, pt. 2 (July 1974), p. 47-74; *Useful plants of Malawi* (Zomba: University of Malawi, 1976); 'A list of some fungi collected in Malawi between 1971 and 1974', *Society of Malawi Journal*, vol. 29, pt. 2 (July 1976), p. 46-53; 'Notes on some changes in the Malawian diet over the last 30 years', *Society of Malawi Journal*, vol. 25, pt. 2 (July 1972), p. 49-54; D. J. Allen, 'Additions to the fungi and plant diseases of Malawi', *Society of Malawi Journal*, vol. 28, pt. 2 (July 1975), p. 35-44.

Memories of the Nyika Plateau.
See item no. 54.

Archaeology

89 Archaeology in Malawi.

J. Desmond Clark. *Society of Malawi Journal*, vol. 19, pt. 2 (July 1966), p. 15-25.

Details the results of the author's work at the north end of the lake to December 1965. He found a wealth of evidence showing habitation there from 60,000 years ago to the present, and was able to date periods of earth movement in the Rift Valley in relation to the history and culture of man back to 3,000 B.C. Other articles by Professor Clark are 'Upper Sangoan industries from Northern Nyasaland and the Luangwa Valley: a case of environment differentiation', *South African Journal of Science*, vol. 50, pt. 8, p. 201-8; and with E. A. Stephens and S. C. Cornydon, 'Pleistocene fossiliferous lake beds of the Malawi (Nyasa) Rift: a preliminary report', *American Anthropologist*, Special Archaeology Number (1966); 'Notes on archaeological work carried out during 1966 in Northern Malawi', *Society of Malawi Journal*, vol. 20, pt. 2 (July 1967), p. 12-16; and 'Prehistoric origins', in *Malawi: the history of a nation* (q.v.), edited by Bridglal Pachai, p. 17-27.

90 Archaeological investigations of a painted rock shelter in Central Malawi.

J. Desmond Clark. *Society of Malawi Journal*, vol. 26, pt. 1 (Jan. 1973), p. 28-46.

This site was in the Chongoni Forest Reserve near Chencherere Hill, eight miles north of Dedza. As well as the rock paintings, tools, potsherds, animal and charcoal remains were discovered and a skeleton was also uncovered, probably a Batwa or Akafula individual. This excavation provided important new evidence about the relationship between hunters and cultivators in the area.

91 Digging for history.

J. Desmond Clark. *Society of Malawi Journal*, vol. 22, pt. 1 (Jan. 1969), p. 52-64.

A lecture by Professor Clark on the contributions of archaeology to African history. 'The archaeologist can add depth and meaning as well as precision to the major part of Malawi history. At the same time he has the responsibility of

Archaeology

making known the results of surveys and informed recognition of finds and the excavation and analysis of specimens by specialists'.

92 Prehistory in Nyasaland.
J. Desmond Clark. *Nyasaland Journal*, vol. 9, pt. 1 (Jan. 1956), p. 92-119.

In 1956 Dr. Clark was curator of the Rhodes-Livingstone Museum in Zambia. Since then he has become professor of archaeology at the University of California at Berkeley and has conducted numerous digs in Malawi. This article is a survey of what was known at that time about local prehistory, and refers to the work of Rodney Wood, W. H. J. Rangeley and Margaret Metcalfe, who has an article, 'Some rock paintings in Nyasaland', in the same number of the journal. Also see *Prehistoric rock art of the Federation of Rhodesia and Nyasaland*, edited by Roger Summers (London: Chatto and Windus, 1959); and 'Malawi' in *Catalogue of fossil hominids. Part I: Africa*, edited by K. P. Oakley and B. G. Campbell (London: Trustees of the British Museum, 1967), p. 31-3.

93 Kukumba Mbiri Mu Malawi, a summary of archaeological research to March, 1973.
Paul A. Cole-King. Zomba, Malawi: Government Press, 1973. 72p. (Department of Antiquities Publication, no. 15).

David Livingstone established the fallacy that Southern Africa had no prehistory, when he observed, 'It is a very remarkable fact, that while in many parts of the world the stone, bronze, and iron instruments of men who have passed away have been found, no flint arrowheads, spears, axes, or other implements of this kind, as far as we can ascertain, have ever been discovered in Africa'. This volume, the result of twenty years' research by a number of scholars, refutes that statement. It contains some excellent plates illustrating various types of pottery found in Malawi, plus a map showing locations of prehistoric sites.

94 Mwalawolemba on Mikolongwe Hill.
Paul A. Cole-King. *Society of Malawi Journal*, vol. 21, pt. 1 (Jan. 1968), p. 34-43.

Cole-King was director of the Museum of Malawi for a number of years. Mikolongwe Hill is one of a series of hills between the Shire Highlands and the Palombe plain to the south; Mwalawolemba is a rock shelter containing schematic rock paintings.

95 The Tertiary and Post-Tertiary lacustrine sediments of the Nyasa Rift Valley.
F. Dixey. *Quarterly Journal of the Geological Society*, vol. 83 (1927), p. 432-45.

Dixey was a government geologist in the 1920s. Among his other works are 'The dinosaur beds of Lake Nyasa', *Transactions of the Royal Society of South Africa*, vol. 16, pt. 1 (1928); 'The Nyasa section of the Great Rift Valley', *Geographical Journal*, vol. 68, p. 133. Also see H. S. Stannus, 'Nyasaland smelting furnace', *Man*, vol. 14 (1914), p. 131-2; P. V. Tobias, 'The men who came before Malawian history', in *Malawi: the history of a nation* (q.v.), edited by Bridglal Pachai, p. 1-16.

96 **Occasional papers, first series.**
Zomba, Malawi: Government Press, 1969. 54p. (Department
of Antiquities Publication, no. 7).

This paperbound pamphlet contains five diverse and interesting articles: 'Malowa
rock shelter', by James Denbow and Richard Ainsworth; 'The burial of Chief
Somba II', by N. D. Kwenje; 'The Matengo settlement', by G. T. Nurse; 'Investigations, mainly of hill sites, carried out in Chief Nyambi's area, Kasupe District', by Lance Klass; and 'A brief history of Joseph Bismarck by himself'.

97 **Occasional papers, second series.**
Zomba, Malawi: Government Press, 1973. 100p. (Department
of Antiquities Publication, no. 14).

The papers are entitled: 'Archaeological investigations along the Nanyangu', by
Hiro Kurashina; 'Zomba range: an early Iron Age site', by Paul A. Cole-King, J.
E. Bushell and J. F. Bushell; and two papers by James Denbow, 'Malowa rock
shelter: archaeological report', and 'Cape Maclear: a preliminary investigation'.

98 **A preliminary report on the recent archaeology of Ngonde,
Northern Malawi.**
K. R. Robinson. *Journal of African History*, vol. 7, pt. 2
(1966), p. 169-88.

A description of a dig near Karonga which concentrated on Mbande Hill, the
ancient capital of the Ngonde under their paramount chiefs, the Kyungu. Three
Iron Age industries were uncovered: the Lufira represented by pottery only; the
Rukuru represented by hut remains, pottery, glass beads, iron, charred millet,
sorghum seeds and bone fragments; and Mbande, characterized by pottery and
beads. The Rukuru beads resembled others, found in Rhodesia, which were
carbon dated to 700 A.D.

99 **The early Iron Age in Malawi: an appraisal.**
K. R. Robinson. Zomba, Malawi: Government Printer,
1969. 10p. (Department of Antiquities Publication, no. 6).

This summary of early fieldwork was followed by a more substantial study, *The
Iron Age of the Upper and Lower Shire, Malawi* (1973). (Department of Anti-
quities Publication, no. 13). Also see B. H. Sandelowsky and K. R. Robinson,
Fingira: a preliminary report (1968), (Department of Antiquities Publication, no.
3) for a report of excavations carried out in 1966 at Fingira Cave on the Nyika
Plateau.

100 **The Iron Age of the southern lake area of Malawi.**
K. R. Robinson. Zomba, Malawi: Government Printer, for
the Department of Antiquities, 1970. 131p.

A report on excavations in 1968 and 1969 in the Fort Johnston District. An Iron
Age site, carbon dated to the 4th century A.D., and overlain with 16th century
Mawudzu ware (the ancestor of modern Cewa pottery), was found at Nkope Bay
near Cape Maclear. Related Iron Age material has been recovered from the
Phopo and Lumbule Hills in Northern Malawi. In addition, see T. Cullen Young,
'A note on iron objects of unknown origin from Northern Nyasaland', *Man*
(1929), p. 147; R. R. Inskeep, 'Recent developments in Iron Age studies in
Northern Rhodesia and Nyasaland', in *Actes du IVe Congrès Pan-Africain de*

Archaeology

Préhistoire, section III, edited by G. Mortelmans and J. Nenquin (Tervuren, Belgium: Musée Royal de l'Afrique Central, 1962), p. 351-6.

101 **The Iron Age of Northern Malawi: recent work.**
K. R. Robinson, B. H. Sandelowsky. *Azania*, vol. 3 (1968), p. 107-46.

Sandelowsky was a student of J. D. Clark at the University of California at Berkeley. This is a report of a 1967 expedition to the Livingstonia-Nyika Plateau areas, where pottery was found similar to the 'dimple-based' ware of East Africa and the channelled ware of Rhodesia, which suggests Malawi was a possible link between the two. See also K. R. Robinson, 'The Iron Age in Malawi: a brief account of recent work', in *Malawi: the history of a nation* (q.v.), edited by Bridglal Pachai; Brian Fagan, 'The Iron Age peoples of Zambia and Malawi', in *Background to evolution in Africa* (Chicago: University of Chicago Press, 1967); R. R. Inskeep, *Preliminary investigation of a proto-historic cemetery at Nkudzi Bay, Malawi* (Lusaka: National Museums of Zambia, 1965. Special Paper).

History

102 **Trade, state and society among the Yao in the 19th century.**
Edward A. Alpers. *Journal of African History*, vol. 10, pt.
3 (1969), p. 405-20.
This article relies on two earlier works, Abdallah's *The Yao* (q.v.), and Duff
MacDonald's *Africana*. Originating in northeastern Mozambique, the Yao were
influenced by the culture of Swahili traders during the 19th century. After con-
verting to Islam, the Yao developed larger political units and turned to slave
trading to build correspondingly stronger economies. In their quest for slaves they
moved into the region around the southern end of Lake Malawi, which they
decimated until defeated by British, Indian and African troops led by Harry
Johnston, Alfred Sharpe and others. Also see E. A. Alpers, *Ivory and slaves in
East and Central Africa* (London: Heinemann, 1975); and 'The Yao in Malawi:
the importance of local research' in *Malawi: the history of a nation* (q.v.), edited
by Bridglal Pachai, p. 168-78; T. Price, 'Yao origins', *Nyasaland Journal*, vol. 17,
pt. 2 (July 1964), p. 11-16; H. S. Stannus, *The Wayao of Nyasaland* (Cambridge, Massachusetts: Harvard University Press, 1922. (Harvard African Studies,
vol. 3)).

103 **Nyasaland, the history of its export trade.**
Colin A. Baker. *Nyasaland Journal*, vol. 15, pt. 1 (Jan.
1962), p. 7-35.
Tobacco, tea, cotton and groundnuts, in that order, dominated the country's trade
during the colonial period. This article covers trading from 1891 to 1960, and
also discusses the development of transportation. Also see the author's 'Malawi's
exports: an economic history', in *Malawi past and present: studies in local and
regional history* (q.v.), edited by Pachai, Smith and Tangri, p. 77-94.

104 **Memoirs of a Malawian.**
Lewis Mataka Bandawe, edited and introduced by Bridglal
Pachai. Blantyre, Malawi: Claim, 1971. 143p.
In 1887, Bandawe was born in Lomwe country in Mozambique. He had a remar-
kable career as a missionary-teacher, an employee of the Nyasaland High Court,
and as a politician with the early Nyasaland African Congress and the Lomwe
Tribal Association.

History

105 **Aibu Chikwenga: an autobiography.**
Aibu Chikwenga, edited by Colin A. Baker. *Society of Malawi Journal*, vol. 25, pt. 2 (July 1972), p. 11-21.

Chikwenga states he was born in 1891, and relates how he travelled with Alfred Sharpe in East Africa just before the First World War, joined the King's African Rifles and fought in both world wars, retired as Regimental Sergeant Major, and then became a member of the Blantyre Urban Court. He wrote, 'I have lived for a long time but I am not really old yet. When some people see me today they think I am a "sheik" from the Moslem church because I wear a Yao hat and have a beard. But most people know that I am a soldier - soldiers do a lot of exercise and keep fit, and that is why I am not really old, even now'.

106 **Kwacha: an autobiography.**
M. W. Kanyama Chiume. Nairobi: East Africa Publishing House, 1975. 247p.

One of the leaders of Malawi's struggle for independence, the author was exiled from the country together with a number of other new ministers a few months after July 1964. Included in this book is his account of those events. Also see Henry Chipembere, 'Malawi in crisis: 1964', *Ufahamu* vol. 1, pt. 2 (1970), p. 1-22.

107 **Lilongwe: a historical study.**
Paul A. Cole-King. Zomba, Malawi: Government Press, 1971. 53p. (Department of Antiquities Publication, no. 10).

Lilongwe was founded as a settlement in 1902. It became the main town of the Central Region, but remained rather small - population 20,000 - until the late 1960s, when it was chosen as the country's new capital. Since then, road building, construction, and a tobacco growing and land development scheme financed by the World Bank, have all contributed to considerable growth and change in the area.

108 **The cancellations of the Rhodesias and Nyasaland.**
H. C. Dann. London: Robson Lowe, 1950. 85p.

A book for philatelists and postal historians. It contains descriptions of 1,335 different stamp cancellations from the earliest days to 1949. Over 150 of these are illustrated. See also *A guide to the postage stamps of the Rhodesias and Nyasaland, 1888-1963* (Salisbury: Mashonaland Philatelic Study Group, 1974).

109 **Nyasaland, the land of the lake.**
Frank Debenham. London: H.M. Stationery Office, 1955. 239p.

One of a series sponsored by the Colonial Office 'to be authoritative and readable, and to give a vivid yet accurate picture', this descriptive survey is by a noted Cambridge geographer.

110 Nyasaland under the Foreign Office.

H. L. Duff. London: George Bell & Sons, 1906. 422p.
Reprinted, New York: Negro Universities Press.

Duff was an official in Alfred Sharpe's administration, and wrote that it was 'impatience of the monotonous life of the cities, impatience of conventional restraints, the love of adventure, the love of sport, the stimulus of the Imperial sentiment, the desire to satisfy an honourable personal ambition', and 'a vague abiding charm, peculiar to the waste places of the earth and to Africa above all others', which attracted Europeans to live there in the early days.

111 The peculiar institution among the early Tumbuka.

C. J. W. Fleming. *Society of Malawi Journal*, vol. 25, pt. 1 (Jan. 1972), p. 5-10.

A short, interesting article on the legal aspects of slavery. Before the late 18th century, it was mainly debtors who became chattels of those to whom their obligation was owed. When Afro-Arab slave dealers penetrated into the interior, wars resulted, and viciousness and brutality reigned.

112 The Zwangendaba succession.

C. J. W. Fleming. *Society of Malawi Journal*, vol. 25, pt. 2 (July 1972), p. 38-48.

Zwangendaba was the Ngoni chief who led his people out of Zululand, across the Limpopo and Zambezi Rivers, into Zambia and Malawi, and then to Mapupo, at the southern end of Lake Tanganyika, where he died in 1848. After his death the unity he had brought to his group disintegrated, and his successors and their followers dispersed and settled in various parts of Malawi, Zambia and Tanzania. See also J. K. Rennie, 'The Ngoni states and European intrusion', in *The Zambesian past: studies in Central African history* (q.v.), edited by Stokes and Brown, p. 302-31; Thomas T. Spear, *Zwangendaba's Ngoni 1821-1890: a political and social history of a migration* (Madison, Wisconsin: University of Wisconsin, 1972. (African Studies Program Occasional Paper, no. 4)); E. H. L. Poole, 'The date of the crossing of the Zambezi by the Ngoni', *Journal of the African Society*, vol. 29 (1930), p. 290-2; R. Codrington, 'The Central Angoniland District of the Protectorate', *Geographical Journal*, vol. 11 (1898), p. 509-22.

113 Adventures in Nyassaland: a two years struggle with Arab slave-dealers in Central Africa.

L. Monteith Fotheringham. London: Sampson Low, Marston, Searle, and Rivington, 1891. 304p.

Fotheringham was the African Lakes Company's agent at Karonga during the wars against Mlozi, and later became company manager in British Central Africa. He had an impenetrable Scots accent and a violent temper, but was the most courageous of all those fighting the slavers. He was motivated by his desire to protect the company's trade interests, and by his great admiration for the Ngonde people, who suffered untold agonies at the hands of Mlozi and his henchmen.

History

114 The Nguru penetration into Nyasaland, 1892-1914.
Thomas Galligan. In: *From Nyasaland to Malawi: studies in colonial history* (q.v.), edited by R. J. Macdonald, p. 108-23.

The Nguru (also called Wakololo but more properly known as Lomwe) originated in Mozambique, east of Lake Chirwa, but were driven from their homeland by famine and by the brutal administration of the Portuguese and the private companies. They took low-paying jobs on the Shire Highlands estates that other Malawians shunned in favour of higher paid work in Rhodesia and South Africa. This was part of the 'ripple effect' of labour emigration in Southern Africa, where workers moved from the poorest areas to the next poorest in a general southward movement.

115 The end of the slave trade in British Central Africa.
Lewis Gann. *Rhodes-Livingstone Journal*, no. 16 (1954), p. 25-51.

Gann argues that the protectorate's naval department played a crucial role in bringing Malawi under government control. He claims that lake steamers compensated for limited manpower and communication difficulties by quickly concentrating forces where they were needed, and by providing a floating artillery barrage which enabled troops to make their assaults on African villages in relative safety. For an early account of the fight against slavers see E. J. Glave, 'Glave in Nyasaland: British raids on the slave raiders', *Century Magazine*, vol. 52 (Aug. 1896); and James Stevenson, 'The Arabs in Central Africa', *Journal of the Manchester Geographical Society*, vol. 4 (1888), p. 72-86.

116 Lakeside pioneers: socio-medical study of Nyasaland, 1875-1920.
Michael Gelfand. Oxford, England: Blackwell, 1964. 330p.

Despite its title, this book by the dean of the University of Rhodesia's medical school covers much more than medical history. It has four chapters on missionary activities and five chapters dealing with the establishment of the colonial government, the suppression of the slave trade, communications, settlers, and labour. The last four chapters deal with medicine - the origins and treatment of jiggers, whooping cough, tuberculosis and other maladies.

117 Livingstone's legacy: the Makololo chiefs of Chikwawa District.
H. G. Graham-Jolly. *Society of Malawi Journal*, vol. 19, pt. 1 (Jan. 1966), p. 7-14.

The Makololo accompanied Livingstone from Lozi country of Western Zambia when he made his transcontinental journey. In 1863 he left them in Southern Malawi where they established themselves as leaders of local people. For many years Graham-Jolly was a colonial civil servant, and he stayed to serve the independent government as its labour officer in Salisbury.

118 **The history of tea in Nyasaland.**
G. G. S. J. Hadlow. *Nyasaland Journal*, vol. 13, pt. 1
(Jan. 1960), p. 21-31.

Henry Brown was the first man to plant tea on a commercial scale in the 1890s.
But it was not until 1908 that it began to pay off, when 23,000 lbs., valued at
£598, were exported, and by 1924 the export value had risen to £1 million.

119 **The beginnings of Nyasaland and north-eastern Rhodesia,**
1859-95.
A. J. Hanna. Oxford, England: Clarendon Press; New
York: Oxford University Press, 1956. 281p.

Hanna was the first professional historian writing about Nyasaland to make use
of primary sources in the records of the British South Africa Company, the
Foreign and Colonial Office correspondence, and various missionary archives.
Although he has been criticized for writing the history of Europeans instead of
Africans in Africa, his work has endured and his general conclusions have not
been successfully challenged.

120 **The story of the Rhodesias and Nyasaland.**
A. J. Hanna. London: Faber, 1960. 288p.

The first attempt to cover this topic in a small, readable volume. It neglects some
important information, particularly Shepperson's work on Chilembwe (q.v.), but
the three chapters on Victorian missionaries and pioneers are useful.

121 **A short history of Karonga.**
P. J. Howson. Zomba, Malawi: Government Printer, 1972.
54p. (Department of Antiquities Publication, no. 11).

During its early history, Karonga was an active ivory and cloth trading centre
because of its road connection with Lake Tanganyika and its African Lakes
Company store. It was disrupted by war from the late 1880s to 1914, when
British and German soldiers fought a battle there.

122 **Livingstone.**
Tim Jeal. London: Heinemann; New York: Putnam, 1973.
427p.

Although primarily a novelist, Jeal wrote this book to coincide with the centenary
of the missionary-explorer's death. As part of the effort to demythologize Livingstone, the book concentrates on his failures as a proselytizer, leader of white men,
husband and father. Also part of this campaign is Judith Listowel's *The other
Livingstone* (London: Julian Friedmann, 1974), which claims that the great man
purposely played down the contributions of four others, W. C. Oswell, László
Magyar, Silva Porto and Candido Cardozo in order to keep all the glory of his
explorations for himself.

123 **The life and letters of Sir Harry Johnston.**
Alex Johnston. New York: Jonathan Cape and Harrison
Smith, 1929. 350p.

Alex was Sir Harry's brother. He relates that Johnston's strategy for dealing with
African and Afro-Arab slavers in British Central Africa was to always battle

them separately and to strike first. Chiefs had to declare their positions unequivocally: Johnston sent them a bullet and some salt. They were expected to indicate peace by returning the salt, or defiance by sending back the bullet.

124 British Central Africa.

Sir Harry Hamilton Johnston. New York: Edward Arnold, 1897. 544p. Reprinted, New York: Negro Universities Press.

This extraordinary book contains over 200 drawings and photographs and demonstrates the wide range of Johnston's talents and interests. Besides being a writer and administrator, he was a noted painter, botanist, ethnologist and linguist. He designed a coat of arms for the Protectorate, coloured in black, yellow, white and red, which features two Africans armed with pick and shovel against a map of Africa, a coffee tree in full bean, and the motto, 'Light in Darkness'.

125 The story of my life.

Sir Harry Hamilton Johnston. London: Chatto & Windus, 1923. 536p.

A vain and snobbish man, Johnston was intensely anti-Semitic, and was often ill. He indulged in many petty jealousies, and ruled over his subordinates with a dictatorial hand. Nevertheless, he was fond of animals and kept a small zoo in Zomba containing serval cats, a leopard, baboons, monkeys, and a variety of birds - especially guinea fowl and crowned cranes, which were left free to roam around his residence.

126 Reality versus romance in South Central Africa.

James Johnston. London: Hodder & Stoughton, 1893. 353p. Reprinted, London: Cass, 1969.

The author was a medical doctor in Jamaica who made a 4,500-mile trek, similar to that of Livingstone, across Southern Africa from Benguela through Lozi country, the Kalahari, Mashonaland, Manica, the Shire Highlands and Lake Nyasa to Chinde at the Zambezi's mouth. In 1969, Cass reissued the book with an introductory essay by James R. Hooker who commented: 'The Scottish author of this book was a somewhat exasperating, rather elusive, but on the whole admirable man.... Instead of projecting the image of a fever-ridden man of God, struggling through harrowing experiences by divine favour, Johnston's reactions (to Southern Africa) seemed to be those of a sensible though somewhat fussy and impatient general practitioner in a backwater village'.

127 My life and the ICU: the autobiography of a black trade unionist in South Africa.

Clements Kadalie. London: Cass; Atlantic Highlands, New Jersey: Humanities Press, 1970. 230p.

Kadalie was a lakeside Tonga, born and raised in Nyasaland. An extraordinary character with an enormous ego, he built the Industrial and Commercial Workers Union of South Africa into an organization of over 100,000 members before it broke on the shoals of tribalism. To obtain a composite view of the man this book should be read along with *Time longer than rope*, edited by Joseph S. Roucek (Madison, Wisconsin: University of Wisconsin Press, 1968).

128 **Trade, the Kyungus, and the emergence of the Ngonde Kingdom of Malawi.**
Owen J. M. Kalinga. *International Journal of African Historical Studies* vol. 12, pt. 1 (1979), p. 17-39.

The author, a lecturer in history at the University of Malawi, questions Godfrey Wilson's thesis that the rise of the Kyungu as rulers of the Ngonde kingdom in Northern Malawi was attributable to long-distance ivory trading. He stresses instead the importance of 'a judicious mixture of religious control and economic exchange, the former probably being of greater political importance, the latter being primarily a result of the organization of the domestic economy' in the development of the state. Also see by Kalinga, 'The establishment and expansion of the Lambya Kingdom c. 1600-1750', *African Studies Review* (Sept. 1978); 'The problem of chronology in the study of Ngonde history', *Malawi Journal of Social Science*, vol. 4 (1975), p. 26-34.

129 **Central Malawi in the 19th century.**
Harry W. Langworthy. In: *From Nyasaland to Malawi: studies in colonial history* (q.v.), edited by R. J. Macdonald, p. 1-43.

The author chose three Cewa areas - Kasungu District, Undi's kingdom in Mchinji and Lilongwe Districts, and Kalonga's sphere of influence along the lake south of Nkhotakota - to illustrate his thesis that, throughout the 19th century, external influences along with changes in the traditional source of wealth brought about political conflicts which resulted in increasing disunity and decentralization in Central Malawi. Also see H. W. Langworthy, 'Chewa or Malawi political organization in the precolonial era', in *Malawi: the history of a nation* (q.v.), edited by Bridglal Pachai, p. 104-22.

130 **Conflict among rulers in the history of Undi's Chewa kingdom.**
Harry W. Langworthy. *Transafrican Journal of History*, vol. 1, pt. 1 (Jan. 1971), p. 1-23.

Although Undi's Cewa kingdom was located in Northwestern Mozambique, this article is pertinent because his was the oldest and most centralized of the major Maravi kingdoms.

131 **Swahili influence in the area between Lake Malawi and the Luangwa River.**
Harry W. Langworthy. *African Historical Studies*, vol. 4, pt. 3 (1971), p. 575-602.

Recounts the late 19th century history of Central Malawi; Swahili influence at Nkhotakota; Swahili-Ngoni relations; and conflicts between the Swahili, Cewa Chief Mwase Kasungu and the British.

History

132 Understanding Malawi's pre-colonial history.

Harry W. Langworthy. *Society of Malawi Journal*, vol. 23, pt. 1 (Jan. 1970), p. 30-47.

While drawing on the earlier works of Rangeley, T. Cullen Young, T. Price, S. J. Ntara and others, the author - professor of history at Cleveland State University - uses his own extensive research on Cewa oral traditions in this article.

133 Ncheu in the 1890s.

M. E. Leslie. *Society of Malawi Journal*, vol. 24, pt. 1 (Jan. 1971), p. 65-78.

Leslie was assistant district commissioner at Ncheu in the 1930s and was acquainted with Paramount Chief of the Ngoni, Philip Gomani. His article draws on interviews with Africans, and on the writings and recollections of various Europeans, to illustrate how tribal officials were elected and how labour was recruited to build roads and work on plantations in the Protectorate.

134 *Mwali* and the Luba origin of the Chewa: some tentative suggestions.

Ian Linden. *Society of Malawi Journal*, vol. 25, pt. 1 (Jan. 1972), p. 11-19.

Mwali was the title of the wife of Karonga, head of the 17th century Maravi empire. The author suggests that the title is cognate with the Luba *Mwadi* and Shona *Mwari*, and characterizes an ancient institution brought east and south by migrant clans from the Lake Kisale area during the 12th to 14th centuries.

135 Catholics, peasants and Chewa resistance in Nyasaland.

Ian Linden, Jane Linden. London: Heinemann; Berkeley, California: University of California Press, 1974. 223p.

This volume tries to balance the emphasis on educated, Protestant élites in early Malawi history by examining the lives of Catholic peasants and the role of *Nyau* societies in resisting missionary influence. Most Catholic Africans were inactive during the colonial period because their priests and nuns, mostly non-British, were anxious to be on their best behaviour in British territory and discouraged political actions by their parishioners.

136 Livingstone's African journal, 1853-1856.

David Livingstone, edited by I. Schapera. London: Chatto & Windus, 1963. 2 vols.

In addition to these volumes, Professor Schapera also edited three other manuscripts: *Livingstone's missionary correspondence, 1841-56*; *David Livingstone: family letters, 1841-56*, 2 vols.; and *Livingstone's private journals, 1851-53*. All this material covers the great missionary's journey up to Lozi country, over to the west coast, and his return to the east coast. Its wealth of detail includes descriptions of the insides of a zebra's stomach and the ritual poisoning of an Angolan chief accused of witchcraft.

137 The rise of our East African empire: early efforts in Nyasaland and Uganda.
Frederick Dealtry Lugard. Edinburgh, London: William Blackwood, 1893. 2 vols. Reprinted, London: Cass, 1968.

In late 1887, Lugard led an expedition against Mlozi at Karonga. In June 1888, while leading an attack, he was shot at point-blank range. The bullet entered his body at the elbow joint of his right arm, struck but did not sever the main artery, entered his chest, glanced off a rib, passed under his chin and came out at the top of his breast pocket, making a long tearing wound at the exit point. Next it struck his left wrist, pulverizing the main bone and cutting a small artery. The single bullet from an Afro-Arab's gun made six holes in Lugard's body. In March 1889, he quit the country. Most of his papers are at Rhodes House, Oxford, but a few are in the Bodleian Library. He wrote three articles about his Central African adventure: 'Lake Nyassa and Central Africa', *Manchester Geographical Society Journal* (1889); 'Nyassaland and its commercial possibilities', *Proceedings of the British Association* (1889); 'The fight against slave-traders', *Contemporary Review* (1889). Also see Margery Perham, *Lugard: the years of adventure, 1858-1898* (London: Collins, 1956).

138 From Nyasaland to Malawi: studies in colonial history.
Edited by Roderick J. Macdonald. Nairobi: East African Publishing House, 1976. 316p.

Contains a number of useful articles on Malawi's colonial history. Each contribution is listed separately in this bibliography under its author's name.

139 The African Lakes Company and the Makololo, 1878-84.
Hugh Macmillan. In: *From Nyasaland to Malawi: studies in colonial history* (q.v.), edited by R. J. Macdonald, p. 65-85.

In 1864, Livingstone left sixteen Makololo porters on the Lower Shire. With the help of their guns, they soon established themselves as rulers of the Mang'anja people on both sides of the river between its confluences with the Ruo and Matope. This article concentrates on their fluctuating relations with the African Lakes Company. Also see the author's 'Notes on the origins of the Arab war', in *Malawi: the history of a nation* (q.v.), edited by Bridglal Pachai, p. 263-82.

140 Kiungani; or, story and history from Central Africa.
A. C. Madan. London: George Bell, 1887. 291p.

Madan translated and edited this book of stories written by boys in Universities' Mission to Central Africa schools on Zanzibar. The youngsters were from fifteen different tribes and almost all had been taken off slave ships by the British east coast anti-slavery squadron. Both 'Nyassa' and Yao groups are represented. A biography of each writer is followed by collections of animal fables from the Lake Victoria, Lake Nyasa and east coast regions.

History

141 **Dr. Albert Thorne's unsuccessful attempt at setting up a black colony in Malawi, 1894-1923.**
M. M. Mapuranga. *Malawi Journal of Social Science*, vol. 5 (1976), p. 44-56.
The author is a history lecturer at the University of Jos, Nigeria. His essay describes a little-known attempt by a Barbadian to repatriate blacks to Africa.

142 **A history of the Malawi police force.**
C. Marlow. Zomba, Malawi: Government Printer, 1971. 42p.
Serious crimes were practically unknown fifty years ago, but in 1921 the Criminal Investigation Department was formed to deal with migrant labourers returning from South Africa and Southern Rhodesia who might have been in contact with criminals in the south.

143 **History and tradition in East Central Africa through the eyes of the Northern Rhodesian Cewa.**
Maxwell Gay Marwick. *Journal of African History*, vol. 4, pt. 3 (1963), p. 375-90.
Despite its emphasis on Northern Rhodesia, this work contains many references to the Cewa of Nyasaland and should be read by anyone interested in Malawi's largest ethnic group. Also see Allen Isaacman, 'The origin, formation and early history of the Chikunda of South Central Africa', *Journal of African History*, vol. 13, pt. 3 (1972), p. 443-61.

144 **Politics and Christianity in Malawi, 1875-1940: the impact of the Livingstonia Mission in the Northern Province.**
John McCracken. London, New York: Cambridge University Press, 1977. 324p. (Cambridge Commonwealth Series).
A revision of the author's 1967 University of Cambridge Ph.D. thesis. It is an outstanding book about Malawi and Livingstonia Mission's tremendous impact on the country during the past century. McCracken is professor of history at University of Stirling, Scotland. Also see his 'Religion and politics in Northern Ngoniland, 1881-1904', in *Malawi: the history of a nation* (q.v.), edited by Bridglal Pachai, p. 215-36.

145 **Underdevelopment in Malawi: the missionary contribution.**
John McCracken. *African Affairs*, no. 303, vol. 76 (April 1977), p. 195-209.
In this study, the author examines the effect of Livingstonia Mission on the economic 'deadness' of Northern Malawi during the colonial period. For other accounts of the mission's first years, see Jaap Van Velsen, 'The missionary factor among the lakeside Tonga of Nyasaland', *Journal of the Rhodes-Livingstone Institute*, no. 26 (Dec. 1959), p. 1-22; Norman Long, 'Bandawe mission station and local politics, 1878-86', *Journal of the Rhodes-Livingstone Institute*, no. 33 (Dec. 1962), p. 1-22; K. J. McCracken, 'Livingstonia as an industrial mission, 1875-1900', in *Religion in Africa* (Edinburgh: University of Edinburgh, Centre of African Studies, 1964), p. 75-96.

34

146 **After Livingstone: an African trade romance.**
Frederick L. M. Moir. London: Hodder & Stoughton,
1926. 200p. Reprinted, Plainview, New York: Books for
Libraries.

The brothers Frederick and John Moir were co-managers of the African Lakes
Company in the 1880s and early 1890s. With its headquarters in Glasgow, the
A.L.C. was the main trading concern in British Central Africa and also one of
the principal transportation companies on the region's lakes and rivers. Closely
connected with the Free Church of Scotland, it shared the same board of direc-
tors with Livingstonia Mission. In 1891, the company was sold to Cecil Rhodes'
British South Africa Company.

147 **The King's African Rifles: a study of the military history of
East and Central Africa, 1890-1945.**
Lt. Col. H. Moyse-Bartlett. Aldershot, England: Gale and
Polden, 1956. 727p.

An extremely detailed account of the King's African Rifles, which developed a
proud military tradition over the years. Nyasaland troops fought other Africans in
colonial struggles in Somaliland, the Gold Coast, and the Gambia, served in their
own region during the First World War, and in India, Madagascar, Ceylon and
Burma during the Second World War. During this time they developed the
custom of being 'first in last out': the first colonial detachment called into a fight
and the last to leave.

148 **Strike a blow and die: a narrative of race relations in
colonial Africa.**
Gideon Simeon Mwase, edited and introduced by Robert I.
Rotberg. Cambridge, Massachusetts; London: Harvard
University Press, 1967. 135p.

Mwase was a storekeeper, government clerk, and politician who served sixteen
months in prison during 1931-32 for embezzling tax money. His story is concerned with race relations, but its most interesting section is devoted to the
Chilembwe Uprising of 1915. Mwase did not know John Chilembwe personally,
but was given his information by Wallace Kampingo, Chilembwe's follower and
fellow inmate at Zomba Central Prison.

149 **Iron Age to independence: a history of Central Africa.**
D. E. Needham. Nairobi, London, New York: Longman,
1974. 208p.

This attractively printed book, containing excellent illustrations and maps, is a
Central African history textbook for use in Zambian secondary schools.

150 **History of the Kamanga tribe of Lake Nyasa.**
Andrew Nkonjera. *Journal of the Royal African Society*,
no. 37, vol. 10 (1910-11), p. 331-41.

The author was a teacher at Livingstonia Mission and his manuscript was
forwarded to the African Society by A. D. Easterbrook, district commissioner for
Central Angoniland. He mentions an earlier article by Dr. Steele of Livingstonia
Mission entitled 'History of the Tambuka' in *Nyasa News* (Aug. 1893).

History

'Kamanga' and 'Tambuka' both refer to the same Northern Malawian ethnic group.

151 Headman's enterprise: an unexpected page in Central African history.
Samuel Josiah Ntara, edited and translated by T. Cullen Young. London: Lutterworth, 1949. 214p.

T. Cullen Young translated, edited and introduced this biography of a Cewa chief. Born around 1830, Chief Msyamboza was a man of originality and intelligence; during his ninety years of life, he saw the coming of the Ngoni from South Africa, the British from Europe, and Dutch Reformed Church missionaries, for whom Ntara worked at Kongwe near Dowa. For a short biography of the author, see Bridglal Pachai, 'Samuel Josiah Ntara', *Society of Malawi Journal*, vol. 21, pt. 2 (July 1968), p. 60-6.

152 The history of the Cewa.
Samuel Josiah Ntara, Harry W. Langworthy. Wiesbaden, German Federal Republic: Franz Steiner Verlag, 1973. 3rd ed. 172p.

Ntara's original work consisted of a series of short narratives recounting traditional histories of Cewa chiefs in Central Malawi. This volume intersperses them with commentaries by Harry W. Langworthy, based on his own field work and that of others, especially W. H. J. Rangeley. The translation of the second edition, which appeared in 1949, is generally regarded as superior to this one.

153 Height and history in Malawi.
G. T. Nurse. Zomba, Malawi: Government Printer, 1969. 39p. (Department of Antiquities Publication, no. 5).

An enquiry into possible historical implications of contrasts in height among Malawians.

154 Ndwandwe and the Ngoni.
G. T. Nurse. *Society of Malawi Journal*, vol. 26, pt. 1 (Jan. 1973), p. 7-14.

A discussion of the origins of the Ngoni Jere and Maseko clans of Malawi and their migration northward from Natal. The author finds it remarkable that after they crossed the Zambezi, they neither fought nor allied with each other, with the exception of a single encounter at Songea in Tanzania. Also see, by the same author, 'The installation of Inkosi ya Makosi Gomani III', *African Music*, vol 4. pt. 1 (1966).

155 The name 'Akafula'.
G. T. Nurse. *Society of Malawi Journal*, vol. 20, pt. 2 (July 1967), p. 17-22.

The Akafula are the race who inhabited Malawi before the coming of the Bantu-speaking peoples. Short in stature and very aggressive, they became keepers of the iron-making furnaces built by the Maravi. Also see W. H. J. Rangeley, 'The earliest inhabitants of Nyasaland', *Nyasaland Journal*, vol. 16, pt. 2 (1963).

156 **The Ntumba.**
    G. T. Nurse. *Society of Malawi Journal*, vol. 30, pt. 2
    (July 1977), p. 11-17.

The only study of the Ntumba, a subdivision of the Cewa, who live among the Ngoni of Ncheu District. The reason for their obscurity lies in their name: the verb *kutumba* means 'capture' and these are the descendents of the captives taken by the Ngoni when they first entered the area.

157 **Sir Harry Johnston and the scramble for Africa.**
    Roland A. Oliver. London: Chatto & Windus, 1957. 368p.

In 1888, Johnston was appointed British Consul to Portuguese East Africa. From 1890 to 1896, he served as commissioner and consul-general for British Central Africa, and administrator for the British South Africa Company's territory north of the Zambezi. Oliver states that many of those who knew him thought of Johnston as a failure. He never learned discretion and his flights of fancy flowed freely even on the most formal occasions and on the most serious subjects. But his gift for taking prompt action in a crisis brought peace to the Protectorate by ending the slave-raiding activities of the Yao, Ngoni and Afro-Arabs. Johnston's papers are in the Salisbury archives with microfilm copies in the library of the Royal Commonwealth Society, London.

158 **The Zulu aftermath: a nineteenth century revolution in Bantu Africa.**
    J. D. Omer-Cooper. London: Longman; Evanston, Illinois:
    Northwestern University Press, 1966. 208p.

A general history of the *Mfecane* or 'time of troubles': the vast dispersion of peoples from Natal into Southern Africa, caused by the military/expansionist policies of the Zulu chief, Shaka. One of the results was the arrival of the Ngoni in the Lake Malawi area in the 1830s. As they settled into the region they created problems for the indigenous Cewa and Tumbuka. Also see H. W. Langworthy and J. D. Omer-Cooper, 'The impact of the Ngoni and the Yao on the 19th century history of Malawi', in *Malawi past and present: studies in local and regional history* (q.v.), edited by Pachai, Smith, and Tangri, p. 15-20.

159 **In the wake of Livingstone and the British administration: some considerations of commerce and Christianity in Malawi.**
    Bridglal Pachai. *Society of Malawi Journal*, vol. 20, pt. 2
    (July 1967), p. 40-69.

Deals with the major consequences of Livingstone's journeys to the Shire Highlands and the lake; the role of missions in opening up the country; and the main issues affecting the relationship between Johnston's administration and the missions and trading companies. Also see Bridglal Pachai, 'Christianity and commerce in Malawi: some pre-colonial and colonial aspects', in *Malawi past and present: studies in local and regional history* (q.v.), edited by Pachai, Smith and Tangri, p. 21-48; and 'The state and churches in Malawi during early Protectorate rule', *Malawi Journal of Social Science*, vol. 1 (1972), p. 7-27.

160 **Livingstone: man of Africa; memorial essays 1873-1973.**
Bridglal Pachai. London, New York: Longman, 1973.
245p.

Contributors to this commemorative volume include Shepperson, McCracken, Schoffeleers, Ross, Gelfand and Page. Individual essays are not listed separately within this bibliography.

161 **The early history of Malawi.**
Edited by Bridglal Pachai. London: Longman; Evanston, Illinois: Northwestern University Press, 1972. 454p.

The title of this book is somewhat misleading since thirteen of the twenty-four chapters deal with the last 100 years of Malawian history. Individual contributions are listed under their author in the relevant sections of this bibliography.

162 **Malawi: the history of a nation.**
Bridglal Pachai. London, New York: Longman, 1973.
324p.

The chapters of this volume originally formed a series of Malawi Broadcasting Company radio talks delivered by the author. The chapter on the 1964 cabinet crisis was edited by Dr. Banda.

163 **The Malawi diaspora and elements of Clements Kadalie.**
Bridglal Pachai. Salisbury: Central Africa Historical Association, 1969. 13f. (Local Series Pamphlet, no. 24).

A series of thumbnail sketches of Kadalie and other Malawian emigrants who achieved prominence in their adopted lands. Among them were E. A. Muwamba of Chinteche - a cousin of Kadalie who became the first African district commissioner in Northern Rhodesia - and Thom Manda of Nkhata Bay, who was among the first Africans appointed to the Northern Rhodesia African Education Advisory Board.

164 **The story of Malawi's capitals: old and new, 1891-1969.**
Bridglal Pachai. *Society of Malawi Journal*, vol. 24, pt. 1 (Jan. 1971), p. 35-56.

Captain Foot, the first British Consul in Central Africa, used Blantyre as his headquarters. His successor, Captain Hawes, decided to move to Zomba because of 'its nearness to the great slave route running from the south end of Lake Nyasa to the Portuguese coast south of Ibo'. The capital remained there from 1886 until 1969, when construction began on the new capital at Lilongwe, in the heartland of the Cewa people. Also see W. J. C. Gerke and C. J. Viljoen, *Master plan for Lilongwe* (Johannesburg: Swan Press, 1968).

165 **Malawi past and present: studies in local and regional history.**
Edited by Bridglal Pachai, Gordon W. Smith, Roger Tangri. Limbe, Malawi: University of Malawi, 1968. 135p.
A collection of papers presented at the University of Malawi's history conference for secondary school teachers, held in June 1967. Each contribution is listed separately under its author in the relevant sections of this bibliography.

166 **The war of *thangata*: Nyasaland and the East African campaign, 1914-18.**
Melvin E. Page. *Journal of African History*, vol. 19, pt. 1 (1978), p. 87-100.
Thangata means 'work which was done without real benefit'. This article examines the role of Malawians as soldiers and military labourers, *tenga-tenga*, during the First World War. Their sufferings during the campaign helped produce the first tentative stirrings of African nationalism. The author is professor of history at Murray State University, Kentucky.

167 **European resistance to African majority rule in Nyasaland: the Settlers' and Residents' Association of Nyasaland, 1960-63.**
Robin H. Palmer. *African Affairs*, no. 271 (1973), p. 256-72.
The Settlers' and Residents' Association of Nyasaland fought a brief, bitter and unsuccessful battle against Malawian nationalism in the early 1960s. After independence, it became obvious that the white population had no cause to fear Dr. Banda's policies, which were designed to create a stable, prosperous African middle class. The author is now a research fellow at Oxford. Also see his 'Johnston and Jameson: a comparative study in the imposition of colonial rule', in *Malawi: the history of a nation* (q.v.), edited by Bridglal Pachai, p. 293-322.

168 **Malawians to remember: John Chilembwe.**
Desmond Dudwa Phiri. Lilongwe, Malawi: Longman, 1976. 106p.
Part of a series intended for both secondary schools and the general public. Other biographies in the series are *Charles Chidongo Chinula* (1975); *James Frederick Sangala* (1974); and *Inkosi Gomani II* (1973). The author, formerly a Ministry of Education official, now runs a correspondence college.

169 **Cultural and political change: the pre-colonial history of Malawi.**
Kings M. Phiri. *Society of Malawi Journal*, vol. 30, pt. 2 (July 1977), p. 6-10.
This essay was presented as a talk to the Society. The author, a history lecturer at the University of Malawi, suggests that, in addition to economic factors, there were cultural determinants of political change during the pre-colonial period. In particular, he mentions developments in Cewa religion which affected politics.

History

170 Pre-colonial economic change in Central Malawi.
Kings M. Phiri. *Malawi Journal of Social Science*, vol. 5 (1976), p. 15-27.

Attempts to show that, between 1750 and the beginning of the colonial era, two systems of exchange emerged as dominant features of pre-colonial Cewa economic organization: one involved the bartering of goods in demand locally, e.g. iron hoes, salt and pots; the other was based on the export of ivory and slaves. Also see the author's 'Early "Malawi" kingship and the dynamics of pre-colonial Chewa society', in *Malawi Journal of Social Science*, vol. 2 (1973), p. 21-30.

171 A pre-colonial history of Malawi.
John G. Pike. *Nyasaland Journal*, vol. 18, pt. 1 (Jan. 1965), p. 22-54.

Pike divides his article into six parts: prehistory from the Kanjeran-Gamblian inter-pluvial period; the coming of the Maravi (Bantu-speaking) peoples, which he dates from the 15th century; the Tumbuka-Nkamanga chiefdom dating from the 18th century; the Ngonde-Nyakyusa settlement in Northern Malawi which was early 18th century; the Ngoni invasions of the 1830s and 1840s; and the coming of the Yao at roughly the same time.

172 Malawi: a political and economic history.
John G. Pike. London: Pall Mall, 1968. 248p. (Pall Mall Library of African Affairs).

Contains useful sections on geography and pre-colonial history. However, the author - a hydrologist turned historian - has neglected the economic history of Malawi, and has overlooked the proto-nationalism that preceded the 1944 Nyasaland African Congress.

173 Nyasaland and Northern Rhodesia: corridor to the North.
Norman H. Pollock, Jr. Pittsburgh, Pennsylvania: Duquesne University Press, 1971. 576p.

Published version of the author's 1948 Ph.D. thesis; it deals adequately with the 1889-1924 period.

174 Doctor on Lake Nyasa: being the journal and letters of Dr. Wordsworth Poole (1895-1897).
Wordsworth Poole, edited by Michael Gelfand. Salisbury: Central African Journal of Medicine, 1961. 70p.

In spite of his relatively brief period in British Central Africa as Harry Johnston's medical officer, Dr. Poole was a sharp and pithy observer of his community while maintaining a paternal interest in Africans.

175 The Central African journal of Lovell J. Procter, 1860-1864.
Lovell J. Procter, edited by Norman R. Bennett, Marguerite Ylvisaker. Boston, Massachusetts: Boston University African Studies Center, 1971. 501p.

The Revd. Procter was a member of the ill-fated first mission to Nyasaland at Magomero, established by Bishop Charles Mackenzie of the Universities' Mission to Central Africa (UMCA). The Revd. Procter was not a strong or dynamic character, but had a talent for recording details of the daily life of the Africans among whom he worked. The original of his journal is held in the papers of the UMCA, at the archives of the United Society for the Propagation of the Gospel in London.

176 **A brief history of the tobacco industry in Nyasaland. Parts I, II, and Additional notes.**
W. H. J. Rangeley. *Nyasaland Journal*, vol. 10, pt. 1 (Jan. 1957), p. 62-83; vol. 10, pt. 2 (July 1957), p. 32-51; vol. 11, pt. 2 (July 1958), p. 24-7.

Rangeley was born at Fort Jameson, became a Rhodes Scholar, joined the colonial administrative service in 1934, and rose to Southern Province commissioner before he died at forty-nine in 1958. Historians are indebted to him for his early research on many topics of continuing interest. John Buchanan introduced tobacco seed into British Central Africa in the early 1890s and since then it has been an economic mainstay. Flue-cured, fire-cured, sun- or air-cured, and burley tobacco are all produced for export. Also see the author's 'Early postal history in the Mlanje area - further comments', and 'The origins of the principal street names of Blantyre and Limbe', in *Nyasaland Journal* vol. 11, pt. 2 (July 1958). Rangeley's papers are held in the Society of Malawi library at the National Museum in Blantyre.

177 **Early Blantyre.**
W. H. J. Rangeley. *Nyasaland Journal*, vol. 7, pt. 1 (Jan. 1954), p. 36-45.

Chronicles the fate of Mtaja, who originally owned much of the land on which the business district of Blantyre now stands. He accumulated considerable wealth from land transactions, had a two-storey house in town, and a coffee plantation at Mulanje managed by a European, but died a pauper as a result of *dagga* smoking and heavy drinking.

178 **Mtwalo.**
W. H. J. Rangeley. *Nyasaland Journal*, vol. 5, pt. 1 (Jan. 1952), p. 55-70.

The history of the Northern Ngoni from 1822 to the early 20th century, when the long-lived Mtwalo II became paramount chief.

179 *Nyau* **in Kotakota District. Parts I and II.**
W. H. J. Rangeley. *Nyasaland Journal*, vol. 2, pt. 2 (July 1949), p. 35-49; vol. 3, pt. 2 (July 1950), p. 19-33.

The *Nyau* danced or put on mimes and small plays at funerals and female initiation ceremonies. These essays contain descriptions of the masks used by this male secret society, some of which are related to Christian teachings. Also see the author's 'Some old Cewa fortresses in the Kotakota District', *Nyasaland Journal*, vol. 4, pt. 1 (Jan. 1951), p. 54-7.

History

180 **Aspects of Central African history.**
Edited by T. O. Ranger. London: Heinemann; Evanston,
Illinois: Northwestern University Press, 1968. 291p.
Written by members of the University College, Dar-es-Salaam, for the use of
Tanzanian high school teachers preparing their students for School Certificate
exams. Contains two chapters by John McCracken, 'The nineteenth century in
Malawi', p. 97-111; and 'African politics in twentieth-century Malawi', p. 190-
209; and one by E. A. Alpers, 'The Mutapa and Malawi political systems', p.
1-28.

181 **Territorial cults in the history of Central Africa.**
T. O. Ranger. *Journal of African History*, vol. 14, pt. 4
(1973), p. 581-97.
A summation of discussions at the Conference on the History of Central African
Religious Systems, held in Lusaka in September 1972. The essay was intended to
be a 'trailer' to the volume *Comparative studies of Central African territorial
cults*, edited by Schoffeleers for Mambo Press, Gwelo, Rhodesia. It is based on
work by Leroy Vail on the Tumbuka, Ian Linden on the shrines of the Karonga
at Mankhamba, and Schoffeleers on the Chisumphi and M'bona cults.

182 **The Zambezi Basin and Nyassaland.**
D. J. Rankin. London: Blackwood, 1893. 277p.
Rankin was a member of the group which accompanied Captain Foot, the first
British Consul to Central Africa in 1883. The author describes the early white
settlers at Blantyre and their relations with local Africans. Also see James
Stevenson, *The civilization of Southeastern Africa including remarks on the
approach to Nyasa by the Zambezi and notes on the country between Kilwa and
Tanganyika* (Glasgow, Scotland: J. Maclehose, 1877). 3rd ed.

183 **The African - a child or a man: the quarrel between the
Blantyre Mission of the Church of Scotland and the British
Central Africa administration, 1890-1905.**
Andrew C. Ross. In: *The Zambesian past: studies in
Central African history* (q.v.), edited by Stokes and Brown,
p. 332-51.
This is a defence of the Blantyre missionaries, led by Alexander Hetherwick.
During what the author calls 'the hysterical period' of 1892-93 'unfair accusations
were made by the missionaries' against the administration. The problem, as
defined by Alfred Sharpe, was that the churchmen resented another political
power dealing with the Africans. Also see the author's 'The political role of the
witchfinder in Southern Malawi during the crisis of October 1964 to May 1965',
in *Witchcraft and healing*, proceedings of a seminar held at the Centre for
African Studies, University of Edinburgh (1969), p. 55-70.

184 **The rise of nationalism in Central Africa: the making of
Malawi and Zambia, 1873-1964.**
Robert I. Rotberg. Cambridge, Massachusetts; London:
Harvard University Press, 1965. 362p.
This well-written work traces the growth of nationalism from its earliest
manifestation - John Chilembwe's uprising - through to the growth of voluntary

associations, religious organizations and workers' strikes, and to the founding of mass political parties and independence. The author teaches at Massachusetts Institute of Technology. Also see Roger Tangri, 'The rise of nationalism in colonial Africa: the case of colonial Malawi', in *Malawi past and present: studies in local and regional history* (q.v.), edited by Pachai, Smith and Tangri, p. 95-113.

185 Gunfire on Nyasa.
G. M. Sanderson. *Nyasaland Journal*, vol. 10, pt. 2 (July 1957), p. 25-31.

A first-hand account of the 'sinking' of the drydocked German lake vessel *Herman von Weissman* by the British lake steamer *Gwendolin* in August 1914 - the first water battle of the First World War. The declaration of war had not yet reached the infuriated German naval commander, who rowed out to the *Gwendolin* shouting 'Gott für damn, vos you dronk?' at the British captain.

186 Central African emergency.
Clyde Sanger. London: Heinemann, 1960. 342p.

The author was a Lusaka-based Canadian newspaper correspondent who was friendly with African nationalists during the 1950s and sympathetic to their cause. His book contains much background information on Nyasaland Congress Party leaders. He relates that, in 1957, Henry Chipembere wanted Dr. Banda to return home to head the party. Chipembere was unhappy with Congress president T. D. T. Banda's inability to force federal members of parliament Wellington Chirwa and Clement Kumbikano to withdraw from the Federal Assembly in protest against the idea of Federation. When Dr. Banda returned to Central Africa from Kumasi, Ghana, where he had been quietly practising medicine, he stopped off in Highfields, Salisbury, where he told a huge crowd, 'To Hell with Federation....If I die my ghost will fight it from the grave'. Sanger claims these were the strongest words the people had heard from an African politician in sixty years.

187 The backbone of Africa: a record of travel during the Great War with some suggestions for administrative reform.
Sir Alfred Sharpe. London: H. F. & G. Witherby, 1921. 232p.

The book records three journeys from Beira to Alexandria. Disappointingly, only one chapter deals with the Protectorate, but Sir Alfred was reticent about his achievements as first governor of Nyasaland. Also see the author's 'Reconstruction in Eastern Africa', *Scottish Geographical Magazine*, vol. 34, pt. 7 (July 1918); 'The backbone of Africa', *Geographical Journal*, vol. 52 (Sept. 1918); 'The geography and economic development of British Central Africa', *Geographical Journal*, vol. 39, pt. 1 (Jan. 1912), p. 1-22; and Robert B. Boeder, 'Sir Alfred Sharpe and the imposition of colonial rule on the Northern Ngoni', *Society of Malawi Journal*, vol. 32, pt. 1 (Jan. 1979), p. 23-30.

History

188 **The *Jumbe* of Kota Kota and some aspects of the history of Islam in British Central Africa.**
George Shepperson. In: *Islam in tropical Africa*, edited by I. M. Lewis. Oxford, England: Oxford University Press, 1966, p. 193-207.
Jumbe was the title of the Swahili rulers of the lakeshore town of Nkhotakota. They governed from the 1840s, when Salim ibn Abdallah first established his influence there, until 1894, when twenty-five-year-old Mwene Kheri was sentenced for murder and sent to Zanzibar.

189 **The military history of British Central Africa.**
George Shepperson. *Rhodes-Livingstone Journal*, no. 26 (1960), p. 23-33.
A review of Lt. Col. H. Moyse-Bartlett's book *The King's African Rifles: a study of the military history of East and Central Africa, 1890-1945* (q.v.), in which the author writes: 'The *machona* (lost ones) of Nyasaland comprise not only those who are torn away from their villages by the pull of the mines and urban life to the south but also that "lost legion" who, as soldiers and carriers, have been dispersed almost all over Africa by military service'.

190 **Independent African.**
George Shepperson, Thomas Price. Edinburgh: University of Edinburgh Press, 1958. 564p.
A biography of John Chilembwe, the American-educated independent churchman whose frustration with bitter arguments about squatters, land rights, and the treatment of African workers led him to attack the Bruce Estates, owned by David Livingstone's grandson, Alexander Livingstone Bruce. Only three Europeans were killed, but Chilembwe and many of his followers were hunted down and shot or hanged. A collection of strange facts and an absorbing tale, the book also provides a fascinating glimpse of the influence of American blacks in early African nationalism. Also see G. Shepperson, 'The place of John Chilembwe in Malawi historiography', in *Malawi: the history of a nation* (q.v.), edited by Bridglal Pachai, p. 405-28; and Robert I. Rotberg, 'Psychological stress and the question of identity: Chilembwe's revolt reconsidered', in *Rebellion in black Africa*, edited by Robert I. Rotberg (London: Oxford University Press, 1971), p. 133-64.

191 **Banda.**
Philip Short. London; Boston, Massachusetts: Routledge & Kegan Paul, 1974. 357p.
An 'unauthorized' biography written by a British journalist with considerable experience in East and Central Africa.

192 **The Zambesian past: studies in Central African history.**
Edited by Eric Stokes, Richard Brown. Manchester, England: Manchester University Press; New York: Humanities Press, 1966. 427p.
Professor Stokes teaches at St. Catherine's College, Cambridge. Individual articles are listed in this bibliography under each author's name.

193 **Fighting the slave hunters in Central Africa: a record of twenty-six years of travel and adventure round the great lakes and of the overthrow of Tip-pu-tib, Rumaliza and other great slave-traders.**
Alfred J. Swann. London: Seeley, 1910. 359p. Reprinted, with an introduction by Norman R. Bennett, London: Cass, 1969.

The author went to Africa in 1882 to captain the London Missionary Society vessels *Good News* and *Morning Star* on Lake Tanganyika and ended his career in 1908 as district resident at Nkhotakota.

194 **Some new aspects of the Nyasaland native rising of 1915.**
Roger Tangri. *African Historical Studies*, vol. 4, pt. 2 (1971), p. 305-13.

Because he knew of his impending deportation to Mauritius, John Chilembwe was forced to initiate his rebellion in haste, which led to its failure.

195 **The Arab War on Lake Nyasa: an account of the campaign against the slaver Mlozi.**
P. T. Terry. *Society of Malawi Journal*, vol. 18, pt. 1 (Jan. 1965), p. 55-77; pt. 2 (July 1965), p. 13-52.

The information in these articles comes from the work of Lugard and Johnston.

196 **Livingstonia, 1875-1975.**
T. J. Thompson. Blantyre, Malawi: Claim, 1975. 16p.

A brief history, with photographs, of the mission's first century. Also see the author's 'African leadership in the Livingstonia Mission, 1875-1900', *Malawi Journal of Social Science*, vol. 2 (1973), p. 76-91.

197 **A history of Central Africa.**
P. E. N. Tindall. London: Longman; New York: Praeger, 1968. 348p.

Ignores the development of 'proto-nationalism' in Nyasaland between the world wars, and concentrates instead on the history of Europeans in the region. See also G. H. Tanser, *A history of Nyasaland* (Johannesburg [n.d.]).

198 **Nyasaland mails and stamps.**
C. D. Twynam. *Nyasaland Journal*, vol. 1, pt. 1 (Jan. 1948), p. 11-25.

The lead article in the journal's first issue. Malawi began with three post offices; by 1948 there were forty-three. The number of articles posted in 1895 was 130,000; by the end of the Second World War it was over four million. On 20 July 1891, Alfred Sharpe, vice consul and acting postmaster, signed the original notification of postage rates. Other essays by the author are 'Incidents in the posts of Nyasaland', *Nyasaland Journal*, vol. 7, pt. 1 (Jan. 1954), p. 46-50; and 'Early postal history of the Mlanje area', *Nyasaland Journal*, vol. 9, pt. 2 (July 1956), p. 21-8. Also see Peter V. Turner, 'Postal history', *Society of Malawi*

History

Journal, vol. 19, pt. 2 (July 1966), p. 52-7; C. A. Baker, 'The postal services in Malawi before 1900', *Society of Malawi Journal*, vol. 24, pt. 1 (July 1971), p. 14-51; J. T. Gosling, 'British Central Africa and its mail system', *St. Martin's-le-Grand Magazine* (1903).

199 The making of an imperial slum: Nyasaland and its railways, 1895-1935.

Leroy Vail. *Journal of African History*, vol. 16, pt. 1 (1975), p. 89-112.

The author, a meticulous scholar, criticizes the Colonial Office's decision to build a railway from Nyasaland to the Indian Ocean. The country suffered from the debt which resulted from the construction. Vail also wrote 'Railway development and colonial underdevelopment: the Nyasaland case', in *The roots of rural poverty in Central and Southern Africa*, edited by Robin Palmer and Neil Parsons (London: Heinemann, 1977), p. 365-95; and 'Nyasaland: paying for railway development', *Empire: a monthly record*, vol. 3, pt. 2 (Feb. 1939), p. 23-5.

200 Notes on the history of the lakeside Tonga of Nyasaland.

Jaap Van Velsen. *African Studies*, vol. 18, pt. 3 (1959), p. 105-17.

'This article is...not only an attempt to reconstruct the pre-1870 period of Tonga history; it is also a description of the way legends and genealogies are manipulated by the various factions to support present claims. At the same time, this is, for the author, an essay in the circumspect use of legends and genealogies in order to learn about the Tonga past and present'.

201 The visit of Her Majesty Queen Elizabeth the Queen Mother to Nyasaland.

Nyasaland Journal, vol. 11, pt. 1 (Jan. 1958), p. 7-22.

The date of this festive occasion was 12-15 July 1957, during a tour of the Federation.

202 Some notes on the history of the Zomba District.

John Watson. *Society of Malawi Journal*, vol. 26, pt. 1 (Jan. 1973), p. 47-59.

Zomba District is the site of Magomero, the first would-be European settlement in the country, and headquarters of the Universities' Mission established in 1861 by Bishop Mackenzie on a bend of the Namadzi River close by the present Land Settlement headquarters at Nasawa. All that remains now are three blue-gum trees and a cross marking the grave of missionary deWint Burrup. The author was Zomba district commissioner from 1949 to 1957, when he became deputy provincial commissioner. Also see Thomas Price, 'Notes on the history of Zomba District', *Society of Malawi Journal*, vol. 27, pt. 1 (Jan. 1974), p. 42-5.

203 An introduction to the history of Central Africa.

A. J. Wills. London, New York: Oxford University Press, 1964. 386p.

The initial three chapters present one of the first attempts to synthesize the Stone Age and Iron Age histories of the region, and a further three chapters provide a concise account of events in the 19th century. However, half the text is devoted

to 20th century colonial developments, and this bias dates the work for readers
interested in African initiatives.

204 **A sailor who did his duty: belated tribute to a real pioneer.**
F. M. Withers. *Nyasaland Journal*, vol. 4, pt. 1 (Jan.
1951), p. 24-39.
The 'real pioneer' is Edward D. Young, 'whose fine work does not appear fully to
have been recognized, or even properly to have been recorded'.

205 **Nyasaland in 1895-96.**
F. M. Withers. *Nyasaland Journal*, vol. 2, pt. 1 (Jan.
1949), p. 16-35.
This essay, and an earlier one by C. A. Cardew, 'Nyasaland in 1894-95', in
Nyasaland Journal, vol. 1, pt. 1 (Jan. 1948), p. 51-5, are richly detailed accounts
of the social and economic aspects of European life in Nyasaland in the 1890s.
Cardew, a pioneer administrator who worked at Liwonde and Ncheu from 1894
to 1921, also wrote 'Nyasaland in the nineties', *Nyasaland Journal*, vol. 8, pt. 1
(Jan. 1955), p. 57-63.

206 **Swahili settlements in northern Zambia and Malawi.**
Marcia Wright, Peter Lary. *African Historical Studies*,
vol. 4, pt. 3 (1971), p. 547-73.
Swahili traders in the Senga-Ngonde areas of Northern Malawi in the 1880s used
two trade routes to the east coast: one was overland via the Nyasa-Tanganyika
corridor to the Mrima coast; the other was across Lake Malawi from Deep Bay
and through Southern Tanzania to Kilwa.

207 **Nyassa: a journal of adventures.**
Edward D. Young, Horace Waller. London, 1877. 239p.
Young was the naval officer in command of the 1875 Free Church of Scotland
expedition which established the first Livingstonia Mission at Cape Maclear. As
well as recounting this event, he describes the lake and the ships which used it.
The Revd. Horace Waller helped write the book and contributed persuasive arguments in favour of an anti-slavery crusade in the area.

208 **The search after Livingstone.**
Edward D. Young. London, 1868. 262p.
Young navigated steamers for Livingstone, during the final two years of his
1858-64 Zambezi expedition. In 1867, when rumours of the missionary's death
reached London, Young was appointed to lead the Royal Geographical Society's
search party. This volume relates the Society's instructions to him and contains
the first accurate description of the north end of Lake Malawi, which he received
from two Afro-Arabs after his Makololo sailors refused to sail through a storm to
the northern shore. Young's article, 'Report of the Livingstone search expedition',
Journal of the Royal Geographical Society, vol. 38 (1868), p. 111-18, is a
shorter version of the book. Also see P. A. Cole-King, *The Livingstone search
expedition, 1867* (Zomba: Government Printer, 1968). (Department of Antiquities
Publication, no. 2).

History

209 Notes on the history of the Tumbuka-Kamanga peoples in the northern province of Nyasaland.
T. Cullen Young. London: R.T.S., 1932. 192p. Reprinted, London: Cass, 1970.

A classic example of oral history. Young was a Livingstonia missionary for twenty years and died in 1955. Also see Leroy Vail, 'Suggestions towards a reinterpreted Tumbuka history', in *Malawi: the history of a nation* (q.v.), edited by Bridglal Pachai, p. 148-67.

Politics in a changing society: a political history of the Fort Jameson Ngoni.
See item no. 348.

The new men revisited: an essay on the development of political consciousness in colonial Malawi.
See item no. 350.

Britain's decolonization policy for Africa, 1945-64: Nyasaland, a case in point.
See item no. 353.

Race and nationalism: the struggle for power in Rhodesia-Nyasaland.
See item no. 354.

The two nations: aspects of the development of race relations in the Rhodesias and Nyasaland.
See item no. 356.

Bandawe mission station and local politics, 1878-86.
See item no. 362.

The politics of African church separatist movements in British Central Africa, 1892-1916.
See item no. 371.

Malawi political systems and the introduction of colonial rule.
See item no. 372.

Colonial and settler pressures and the African move to the politics of representation and union in Nyasaland.
See item no. 373.

Some early pressure groups in Malawi.
See item no. 375.

Religion

210 *Achirwa* - one of us: a memoir of Christopher Lacey, O.B.E.,
archdeacon.
Blantyre, Malawi: Anglican Diocese of Malawi, 1969. 29p.
Extremely courteous and outwardly very eccentric, Lacey went out to Malawi in
1937 and died there, thirty-one years later, after serving the church on Likoma
Island and in Southern Region. The Blantyre *Times* wrote: 'Hundreds of people
of all races will miss his valuable advice and counsel, his cheerfulness and that
love which he so delightedly bestowed upon everyone with whom he came in
contact'.

211 Thirty years in Nyasaland.
Augustine Ambali. London: Universities' Mission to
Central Africa, 1931. 63p.
Ambali was born on the east coast, forcibly circumcised as a Moslem, sold into
slavery, freed by the British anti-slavery squadron, converted to Christianity, and
brought to Nyasaland by the Revd. W. P. Johnson. He spent forty-six years
there, and became Canon of Likoma and Priest-in-Charge of Msumba Bay and
Ngoo Bay.

212 The history of the Universities' Mission to Central Africa,
1859-1965.
A. E. M. Anderson-Morshead, A. G. Blood. London:
Universities' Mission to Central Africa, 1955-62. 3 vols. and
supplement.
Volume I relates the story of the accidental death by drowning on Lake Malawi
of Bishop Chauncey Maples. For more on the Universities' Mission to Central
Africa see Revd. P. Elston, 'A note on the Universities' Mission to Central
Africa, 1859-1914', in *Malawi: the history of a nation* (q.v.), edited by Bridglal
Pachai, p. 344-64.

Religion

213 **Slave-boy to priest.**
C. W. B. Arnold. *Nyasaland Journal*, vol. 2, pt. 1 (Jan.
1949), p. 7-14.
Tells of the Revd. Petro Kilekwa, who was born a Bisa in Northern Rhodesia,
captured as a small child in 1881, freed a few years later, enlisted by the Royal
Navy, and was eventually ordained as an Anglican priest on Likoma Island in
1917. His story was published in English under the above title (London: Universities' Mission to Central Africa, 1937).

214 **Johnson of Nyasaland: a study of the life and work of
William Percival Johnson, D.D.**
Bertram Herbert Barnes. London: Universities' Mission to
Central Africa, 1933. 258p.
The author was an Anglican priest who worked with Johnson for several years.
Johnson lived in Africa from 1876 to 1928; most of that time he was blind in one
eye and had no night vision in the other. Despite this handicap, he learned to
read Arabic and often carried the Koran as well as the Bible. He spent a good
deal of time travelling through Northern Mozambique between Lake Malawi and
the Indian Ocean, and knew the slave routes of that region particularly well.

215 **The diary of a working man.**
William Bellingham, edited by J. C. Yarborough. London:
Society for the Promotion of Christian Knowledge, 1888.
141p.
Bellingham was a mission worker employed to reconstruct ships on the lake.

216 **Kristofa's adventures on Lake Nyasa.**
Mary Winifred Bulley. London: Universities' Mission to
Central Africa [1920]. 48p.
An unusual book written to teach children about the work of the U.M.C.A. in
Central Africa. It tells the story of an African boy who came in contact with the
mission, and was taught, baptized, became a priest and finally a missionary in
Northern Rhodesia. Each chapter includes play sheets and pictures which can be
cut out and assembled.

217 **Lonely warrior.**
George H. Campbell. Blantyre, Malawi: Claim, 1975. 62p.
A biography of William Koyi, who was born in 1846 in Cape Province, South
Africa. He became a Christian, was educated at Lovedale Institution of the Free
Church of Scotland, and in 1876 volunteered to go to Malawi with a missionary
party headed by James Stewart. Since he spoke Zulu he was particularly effective
in proselytizing among the Ngoni. He died in 1886 and was buried at Njuyu in
Northern Region.

218 **The Blantyre missionaries: discreditable disclosures.**
A. Chirnside. London: William Ridgway, 1880. 24p.
The early Church of Scotland missionaries were not very successful; and in their
eagerness to obtain converts they often tried to force change on the local people.
This alienated the Africans and also brought criticism from the home mission

board. Such objections prompted this book and another by A. Riddel, *A reply to 'The Blantyre missionaries: discreditable disclosures'* (Edinburgh: W. Blackwood, 1880).

219 **The influence of Livingstonia Mission upon the formation of welfare associations in Zambia, 1912-31.**
David J. Cook. In: *Themes in the Christian history of Central Africa* (q.v.), edited by T. Ranger and J. Weller, p. 98-134.
President Kaunda's father, the Revd. David Kaunda, was educated at Livingstonia and founded Lubwa Mission in Chinsali District, Northern Province of Zambia, and also set up the first schools and church. The first mission established by Livingstonia in Northeastern Rhodesia was at Mwenzo, on the Stevenson Road. In 1912 school inspector Donald Siwale formed the first welfare association at Mwenzo, and at the same time his school friend Levi Mumba founded the North Nyasa Native Association.

220 **Darkness or light.**
Godfrey Dale. London: Universities' Mission to Central Africa, 1925. 3rd ed. 280p.
First published in 1912, this book describes the work of the Universities' Mission to Central Africa in Zanzibar, on Lake Malawi and in Zambia. It contains chapters on Islam in Africa, the mission's medical work, and descriptions of the difficulties encountered by early missionaries.

221 **Among the wild Ngoni.**
W. A. Elmslie. London: Oliphant, Anderson & Ferrier, 1899. 320p. Reprinted, London: Frank Cass, 1970.
A medical missionary, Elmslie worked with Donald Fraser, Charles Stuart, and William Koyi among the Northern Ngoni at Ekwendeni. The book includes a brief history of the Ngoni, and traces them back to their days as part of Shaka's impis and their subsequent northward migration. It was the self-appointed task of these early missionaries to make the Ngoni abjure violence and to separate them from their subject Tumbuka and Tonga peoples.

222 **Donald Fraser of Livingstonia.**
Agnes R. Fraser. London: Hodder & Stoughton, 1934. 325p.
One of the founders of the Student Christian Movement in Britain, Dr. Fraser worked among the Northern Ngoni, helping to bring them under colonial government supervision without bloodshed.

223 **Livingstonia: the story of our mission.**
Donald Fraser. Edinburgh: Foreign Mission Committee of the United Free Church of Scotland, 1915. 88p.
Includes photos of mission and African life, and contains a list of those who served at Livingstonia from 1875 to 1914.

Religion

224 **Winning a primitive people: sixteen years' work among the warlike tribe of the Ngoni and the Senga and Tumbuka peoples of Central Africa.**
Donald Fraser. London: Seeley Service, 1922. 320p.
Reprinted, New York: Negro Universities Press.
This book established Fraser's reputation as an authority on Northern Nyasaland. His other works include *The future of Africa* (1911); *African idylls* (1923); *Autobiography of an African* (1925); and *The new Africa* (1927).

225 **Memoir of Bishop Mackenzie.**
Harvey Goodwin. Cambridge, England: Deighton, Bell, 1864. 438p.
Written by the Dean of Ely, who made use of Mackenzie's private letters and other materials provided by his family. The Bishop served in Natal before embarking on his ill-fated attempt to set up Malawi's first Christian mission at Magomero. He died of a combination of dysentery, maleria and exposure on 31 January 1862, on an island at the confluence of the Ruo and Shire Rivers.

226 **Blantyre Mission.**
Stephen Green. *Nyasaland Journal*, vol. 10, pt. 2 (July 1957), p. 6-17.
The Church of Scotland Mission at Blantyre was founded in 1867, and construction of its famous church began in 1888. In 1925 the Presbyteries of the Livingstonia Free Church of Scotland and Blantyre joined to form the Synod of the Church of Central Africa Presbyterian, and two years later they were joined by the Dutch Reformed Church.

227 **The Nyasaland government's policy towards African Muslims, 1900-25.**
Robert Greenstein. In: *From Nyasaland to Malawi: studies in colonial history* (q.v.), edited by R. J. Macdonald, p. 144-68.
Despite charges of anti-clericalism from Christian missionaries the colonial administration generally adopted a neutral or pragmatic stand toward the spread of Islam. Moslem Yao were faithful and dependable workers who were favoured by administrators such as Sharpe, Swann and George Smith. For criticisms of the government's policy see Alexander Hetherwick, 'Islam and Christianity in Nyasaland', *Muslim World*, vol. 17 (1927); A. C. Van Wyk, 'Mohammedanism in Nyasaland today', *Muslim World*, vol. 24 (1934); and A. L. Hofmeyr, 'Islam in Nyasaland', *Muslim World*, vol. 2 (1912).

228 **Forerunners of modern Malawi.**
James Henderson, edited by M. M. S. Ballantyne, R. H. W. Shepherd. Lovedale, South Africa: Lovedale Press, 1968. 301p.
The letters of the Revd. James Henderson, a Livingstonia missionary, to his fiancée, Margaret Davidson, 1895-98. After their marriage he became head of the Training School at Overtoun Institution, Livingstonia, and then replaced the Revd. Stewart as principal of Lovedale Missionary Institution in South Africa.

229 Robert Hellier Napier in Nyasaland.
Edited by Alexander Hetherwick. London: William
Blackwood, 1925. 158p.

Napier served as a Church of Scotland missionary from 1909 until 1914 when he
joined the British army in East Africa. Eventually he became its chief scout and
intelligence officer. He was exceptionally daring in this role and, on 12 February
1918, was killed in Mozambique during an encounter with a German advance
patrol.

230 The building of the Blantyre church, Nyasaland, 1888-1891.
Alexander Hetherwick. Blantyre, Malawi: Blantyre Synod
Bookshop, 1962. 23p.

Before beginningthe Blantyre church, the Revd. D. C. Scott - who later constructed the magnificent Church of St. Michael and All Angels - had no building
or architectural experience. Also see Denis M'Passou, *Likoma Cathedral: the
story of St. Peter's Cathedral* (Zomba: Anglican Council in Malawi [n.d.]).

231 The Gospel and the African.
Alexander Hetherwick. Edinburgh: T. & T. Clark;
Naperville, Illinois: Allenson, 1932. 176p.

The Croall Lectures for 1930-31 on the impact of the gospel on Central Africa.
The lectures include 'Native mentality and environment', 'Native beliefs', 'Shad-
ows and fears', 'The appeal through native beliefs', 'How the seed is best sown',
and 'Problems to be faced'.

232 The romance of Blantyre: how Livingstone's dream came true.
Alexander Hetherwick. London: James Clarke [1931].
260p.

For many years Hetherwick and Robert Laws were the leading missionaries in
the country. Hetherwick was a prominent freemason and an opponent of the
'Roman' missionaries; from 1883 to 1928, he presided over the development of
Blantyre Mission, its school, printing press, and cathedral. Also see Revd. Wil-
liam Robertson, *The martyrs of Blantyre: Henry Henderson, Dr. John Bowie,
Robert Cleland* (London: James Nisbet, 1892). In 1888, Cleland was the first
European to climb Mt. Mulanje. Also see Revd. T. Cheeseman, *The story of
William Trelfall, missionary martyr of Nyasaland* (1910).

233 Witnesses and Watchtower in the Rhodesias and Nyasaland.
James R. Hooker. *Journal of African History*, vol. 6, pt. 1
(1965), p. 91-106.

The Central African branch of the Jehovah's Witnesses believed that Satan ruled
the earth through commercial, political and religious instruments. Consequently,
'Witnesses' or 'Watchtowerites' refused to have anything to do with colonial
administrators and Europeans generally. They were kept under surveillance during
pre-independence days, but were not oppressed since they were conservative,
hard-working and apolitical. Professor Hooker predicts the independent government may have problems with the Witnesses. For a discussion of recent events see
'Jehovah's Witnesses in Malawi', *Africa Report*, vol. 21, pt. 1 (Jan.-Feb. 1976),
p. 37-9 and *Awake*, (8 Dec. 1975).

Religion

234 Daybreak in Livingstonia.
James W. Jack. Edinburgh: Oliphant, Anderson & Ferrier, 1901. 371p.

Introduced by Dr. Laws, who praises the Revd. Jack's mastery of detail although the author had never visited Nyasaland. The author states: 'One of the main objects of the Mission would be to assist, by means of the Gospel, in the extinguishing of the accursed slave-trade in that region - certainly a blessed and Christlike object. Its promoters realized that there could be no more powerful remedy for this evil than the Gospel of Jesus, before which all evils must vanish as chilling icebergs before warm currents and summer skies. But the highest object in the foundation of the Mission was to make known the glad tidings of a Saviour to the ignorant and superstitious children of Nyasa. It was to hold forth the light of the Gospel. What the colossal Statue of Liberty, at the head of New York harbour, is to mariners on a dark night, the Livingstonia Mission was to be in a spiritual and far higher sense to the natives in Central Africa'.

235 My African reminiscences 1876-1895.
William Percival Johnson. London: Universities' Mission to Central Africa, 1926. 236p. Reprinted, New York: Negro Universities Press.

Johnson was an Oxford scholar who became a U.M.C.A. missionary and worked alone on the eastern shore of Lake Malawi for several years before the Likoma Island mission station opened. His self-effacing account of his work is well supplemented by B. H. Barnes' *Johnson of Nyasaland: a study of the life and work of William Percival Johnson, D.D.* (q.v.), which gives Johnson full credit for developing the 'moving ministry' - the use of lake steamers to spread the Gospel. Barnes also describes Johnson's efforts to convert the largely Moslem lake peoples. Also see D. Y. Mills, *A hero man: the life and adventures of William Percival Johnson, Archdeacon of Nyasa* (London: U.M.C.A., 1931).

236 Nyasa the great water.
William P. Johnson. London, New York: Oxford University Press, 1922. 204p. Reprinted, New York: Negro Universities Press.

Although described as a poor speaker, unable to express his own ideas, Johnson wrote books, including this storehouse of historical and sociological material about the lake. Also see his *The Psalms in Nyasaland* (Cardiff, England: Smith Brothers, 1923).

237 Traditional religion among the Tumbuka and other tribes.
Steven Kauta. *Ministry*, vol. 9, pt. 1 (Jan. 1969), p. 1-6.

The Revd. Kauta was a Church of Central Africa Presbyterian clergyman who tried to prove that all Malawi's traditional religions were monotheistic, and used one word for God, 'Leza', which means 'he who looks after children'. As well as Leza, however, there was a complex system of spirit messengers who relayed human needs to God. These spirits also visited each other, married, and fought; the signs of their struggles were heavy storms, thunder and lightning. Female seers or prophetesses were another feature of many Malawian religions.

238 **The Zambesi journal and letters of Dr. John Kirk, 1858-63.**
John Kirk, edited by Reginald Foskett. Edinburgh: Oliver
& Boyd, 1965. 2 vols.
Kirk was more objective and less enthusiastic than Livingstone about the possibilities of a 'civilizing mission' in Central Africa. Had these diaries been available in the 1870s, his descriptions of changing river depths and channels, sudden lake storms, corrosive river water, shifting sand bars, and difficulties of locating efficient steamer fuel would have discouraged the reader from using the Zambezi route as an access to Lake Malawi.

239 **Chewa initiation rites and *Nyau* societies: the use of religious institutions in local politics at Mua.**
Ian Linden. In: *Themes in the Christian history of Central Africa* (q.v.), edited by T. O. Ranger and J. Weller, p. 30-44.
Mua is a Roman Catholic mission located on the plain near the southern end of the lake. *Nyau* secret societies were a central feature of Cewa culture for hundreds of years. Their dancers participated in all the major rites of transition, from birth through initiation to death.

240 **John Chilembwe and the New Jerusalem.**
Ian Linden, Jane Linden. *Journal of African History*, vol. 12, pt. 4 (1971), p. 629-51.
An analysis of the 1915 Chilembwe rising within the context of millennial belief. The author attempts to show how a development from Passionism to activism from October 1914 to January 1915 was the proximate cause of open revolt. Also see the authors' 'Chiefs and pastors in the Ncheu rising of 1915', in *From Nyasaland to Malawi: studies in colonial history* (q.v.), edited by R. Macdonald, p. 169-88.

241 **A prince of missionaries.**
W. P. Livingstone. London: James Clarke [1931]. 206p.
A 'popular sketch' of the life and work of the Revd. Alexander Hetherwick. The author praises his subject as a 'seer and statesman and spiritual genius' and emphasizes Hetherwick's sympathy for Africans. He notes that Hetherwick's biography 'might well form a text-book on the development of the relations between Black and White'.

242 **Laws of Livingstonia.**
W. P. Livingstone. London: Hodder & Stoughton [1921]. 385p.
A tribute to a man regarded as a saint by his co-workers, which went through three editions in its first two years of publication. Also see Robert Laws, *Reminiscences of Livingstonia* (London, 1934).

Religion

243 Joseph Booth, Charles Domingo, and the Seventh Day Baptists in Northern Nyasaland, 1910-12.
Kenneth P. Lohrentz. *Journal of African History*, vol. 12, pt. 3 (1971), p. 461-80.

Draws on previously undiscovered material in the archives of the Seventh Day Baptist Historical Society and the *Sabbath Recorder*. This magazine is associated with the Sabbath Evangelizing and Industrial Association of Plainfield, New Jersey, one of the many groups Booth was associated with during his varied career.

244 Tonga religious beliefs and customs. Parts I and II.
Alexander G. MacAlpine. *Journal of the African Society*, no. 19, vol. 5 (1906), p. 187-90, 257-68, 377-80; no. 24, vol. 6 (1906-07), p. 375-84.

For many years MacAlpine was a Livingstonia missionary southwest of Bandawe, and during this time he collected what he called 'old heathen customs'. He discusses rites surrounding death; spirits (intercourse between the living and the dead was believed possible); various medicines; God - called 'Chiuta', the wonder-worker; and forms of worship.

245 Africana, or the heart of heathen Africa.
Duff MacDonald. Edinburgh: John Menzies, 1881. 2 vols. Reprinted, New York: Negro Universities Press.

MacDonald was a missionary who was dismissed following the 1881 Blantyre Mission scandal. Volume one discusses 'Native customs and beliefs', and volume two is devoted to mission life. Included are chapters on African law, government, witchcraft, philology and a fifty-page appendix of African folk tales.

246 Religious independency as a means of social advance in Northern Nyasaland in the 1930s.
Roderick J. Macdonald. *Journal of Religion in Africa*, vol. 3, pt. 2 (1970), p. 106-29.

A discussion of the establishment and development of several churches in Northern Malawi from 1926 to 1935, and of the close interaction among key personalities, many of whom were Tongas and were closely related. Much of the article is devoted to the Revd. Yesaya Zerenje Mwasi, 'a man of boundless ambition', and the various organizations he supported.

247 Rev. Dr. Daniel Sharpe Malekebu and the re-opening of the Providence Industrial Mission: 1926-39.
Roderick J. Macdonald. In: *From Nyasaland to Malawi: studies in colonial history* (q.v.), edited by R. J. Macdonald, p. 215-33.

Apart from Dr. Malekebu's own work, *My vision: East Central and South Africa of today* (Foreign Mission Board, 1950), this is the only biography of John Chilembwe's successor at Providence Industrial Mission. Dr. Malekebu received his medical degree at Meharry Medical College in Nashville, Tennessee, but - unlike Dr. Banda - he chose to remain a clergyman, doctor and educator rather than becoming a politician.

248 **Reverend Hanock Msokera Phiri and the establishment in Nyasaland of the African Methodist Episcopal Church.**
Roderick J. Macdonald. *African Historical Studies*, vol. 3, pt. 1 (1970), p. 75-87.
The Revd. Phiri, Dr. Banda's uncle, first joined the African Methodist Episcopal Church in South Africa in 1923. While there, he became acquainted with the black American Bishop William Tecumseh Vernon, who was responsible for bringing the young Kamuzu to the U.S.A. The Revd. Phiri set up A.M.E. schools and churches in Northern Rhodesia, Tanganyika, and Katanga, as well as in Malawi.

249 **Journals and papers of Chauncey Maples.**
Chauncey Maples, edited by Ellen Maples. London: Longman, Green & Co., 1899. 278p.
Begins with Bishop Maples' account of his 1882 journey through 900 miles of Makua country in the northeastern corner of Mozambique, and describes his subsequent period as leader of the Universities' Mission to Central Africa mission on Likoma Island. Included are his *Nyasa News* articles from 1893 to 1895, documenting his attempts to convert the Moslem Yao to Christianity. Ellen Maples published a biography of her brother entitled *Chauncey Maples* (London: Longman, 1897).

250 **Time to remember: the story of the Diocese of Nyasaland.**
Mary McCulloch. London: Universities' Mission to Central Africa, 1959. 123p.
The memoirs of the author's many years as an Anglican missionary at Malosa, near Zomba.

251 **What we do in Nyasaland.**
Edited by Dora Yarnton Mills. London: Universities' Mission to Central Africa, 1911. 266p.
A collection of essays written by missionaries about the U.M.C.A.'s unique floating missions. They describe life aboard the mission steamers, the responsibilities of African and European crew members, the missionaries and their African assistants, and their successes and failures.

252 **Streams in the desert: a picture of life in Livingstonia.**
J. H. Morrison. London: Hodder & Stoughton [1919]. 174p. Reprinted, New York: Negro Universities Press, 1969.
The author calls this 'a simple narrative of a long week-end in Central Africa spent in continuous travelling among the various tribes of Nyasaland and northeastern Rhodesia.... Contact with the natives in their villages and along their forest paths brought a supreme and astonishing revelation of the humanness and lovableness of the African. Some impression of this it has been my main endeavour to convey to the reader'.

Religion

253 Missions and politics in Malawi.
K. Nyamayaro Mufuka. Kingston, Canada: Limestone Press, 1977. 289p.

Professor Mufuka teaches in the history department of Lander College in Greenwood, South Carolina. This book tends to generalize about the work of Scots missionaries in the country, and make wide-ranging comparisons with mission history in other African countries.

254 Particulars of 50 marriage cases in the Diocese of Nyasaland together with the reports of the assessors and the decisions made thereupon.
Likoma, Malawi: Universities' Mission Press, 1926. 129p.

These were divorce cases judged by the Anglican Bishop Cathrew Fisher of Likoma Island. The book's purpose was to establish legal principles to guide priests through the difficulties of the 'Laws of Christian Marriage'. Decisions were made under rules drawn up in the Synod of 1922. For comparison, see G. N. Hochstenbach, 'Towards a true Christianization of marriage and family life in the Lower Shire Valley of Malawi', an essay submitted for the Diploma of Pastoral Studies, Pastoral Institute of Eastern Africa, Gaba, Ethiopia, 1968.

255 The story of the Dutch Reformed Church Mission in Nyasaland.
J. L. Pretorious. *Nyasaland Journal*, vol. 10, pt. 1 (Jan. 1957), p. 11-22.

Compared with the extensive writings on other missions in the country the D.R.C. has been virtually ignored, perhaps due to the conservatism of its clergy and their ties with South Africa. The church began its work in Malawi in 1889 under the Revd. A. C. Murray, and its African converts become members of the Synod of the Church of Central Africa Presbyterian - not of the Synod of the D.R.C. of South Africa. The author was principal of Milliam Murray Teacher Training College at Mkhoma Mission for many years, served as a federal member of parliament, and died in Blantyre in 1968. See his 'An introduction to the history of the Dutch Reformed Church Mission in Malawi, 1889-1914', in *Malawi: the history of a nation* (q.v.), edited by Bridglal Pachai, p. 365-83.

256 Arthur Douglas, missionary on Lake Nyasa: the story of his life.
B. W. Randolph. London: Universities' Mission to Central Africa, 1920. 312p.

Douglas was an Anglican missionary, and worked at Nkhotakota, Likoma Island, and St. Michael's College at Kango, Mozambique, from 1901 to 1911. In that year he was shot to death by a Portuguese corporal, apparently because he had protected some African girls from sexual assaults by another Portuguese.

257 Nyasaland rain shrines.
W. H. J. Rangeley. *Nyasaland Journal*, vol. 5, pt. 2 (July 1952), p. 31-50.

Based on interviews with Samuel Ntara and others, the article discusses the 'rain makers' of the Phiri clan of the Cewa - the first Bantu-speaking inhabitants of Malawi. Makewana, mother of all people, is the subject of this article while

M'Bona, guardian spirit of all people, is the subject of 'M'Bona - the rain maker', in *Nyasaland Journal*, vol. 6, pt. 1 (Jan. 1953), p. 8-27. B. J. Kathamalo's 'Khulubvi Thicket - Port Herald', *Society of Malawi Journal*, vol. 18, pt. 2 (July 1965), p. 53-4, is a short discussion of the kinds of vegetation in M'Bona's place of worship.

258 **The historical study of African religion.**
Edited by T. O. Ranger, Isaria Kimambo. London:
Heinemann; Berkeley, California: University of California
Press, 1972. 320p.
Individual articles are listed under their authors' names in the relevant sections of this bibliography.

259 **Themes in the Christian history of Central Africa.**
Edited by T. O. Ranger, John C. Weller. London:
Heinemann; Berkeley, California: University of California
Press, 1975. 285p.
Individual articles are listed under their authors' names in the relevant sections of this bibliography.

260 **A hero of the Dark Continent: memoir of Rev. Wm. Affleck Scott.**
W. Henry Rankine. London: William Blackwood, 1896.
313p.
W. A. Scott was a Church of Scotland missionary doctor at Blantyre from 1889 to 1895, when he died of malaria. His brother, the Revd. D. C. Scott, was also there as head of the mission. (There was a Dr. Henry E. Scott attached to the Church of Scotland mission at Domasi but he was no relation.) W. A. Scott died young, but this was quite common in the early days; disease, poor diet, and the rigours of a strange climate claimed many of the first Europeans.

261 **The story of the Universities' Mission to Central Africa, from its commencement under Bishop Mackenzie to its withdrawal from the Zambezi.**
Henry Rowley. London, 1867. Reprinted, New York:
Negro Universities Press, 1969.
This is Rowley's journal of his life at Magomero with Bishop Mackenzie and others. Also see Revd. G. H. Wilson, *A missionary's life in Nyasaland* (London: Universities' Mission to Central Africa, [n.d.]); Owen Chadwick, *Mackenzie's grave* (London, 1959); and J. E. R. Emtage, 'The first mission settlement in Nyasaland', *Nyasaland Journal*, vol. 8, pt. 1 (Jan. 1955), p. 16-24, which contains much the same information as does the Rowley volume.

Religion

262 **The history and political role of the M'Bona cult among the Manganja.**
Matthew Schoffeleers. In: *The historical study of African religion* (q.v.), edited by T. O. Ranger and I. Kimambo, p. 73-94.

Schoffeleers sees similarities between the extent of influence, ideologies, external organizations, and relationships with the local socio-political structures, in the cases of the M'Bona shrine at Khulubvi near the Shire River town of Nsanje in Southern Malawi; the Mwari, Chaminuka and Dzivaguru cults south of the Zambezi; and the Chauta and Chisumphi cults of the northern and western sections of the Maravi confederation. He suggests that a treatment of this complex of religious cults might be fruitful. Also see J. P. Bruwer's two articles, 'Notes on Maravi origin and migration', *African Studies*, vol. 9, pt. 1 (1950), p. 32-4; and 'Remnants of a rain cult among the Acewa', *African Studies*, vol. 11, pt. 4 (Dec. 1952), p. 179-82.

263 **The interaction of the M'Bona cult and Christianity, 1859-1963.**
Matthew Schoffeleers. In: *Themes in the Christian history of Central Africa* (q.v.), edited by T. O. Ranger and J. Weller, p. 14-29.

It was believed that many centuries ago, the spirit of the High God visited shrines at Thyolo and Khulubvi in the wind and manifested itself in the form of a great snake. A human girl-wife, known as M'Bona, was provided for the spirit and acted as an intermediary, articulating God's commands. Christian missionaries were opposed to the M'Bona cult, but many Southern Malawians believed there were parallels between the lives of Christ and M'Bona.

264 **The resistance of the *Nyau* societies to the Roman Catholic missions in colonial Malawi.**
Matthew Schoffeleers, Ian Linden. In: *The historical study of African religion* (q.v.), edited by T. O. Ranger and I. Kimambo, p. 252-73.

The authors chose to study Roman Catholic missions because of their own personal knowledge of them and because of the special liturgical and institutional aspects of Catholicism which have interesting parallels with the *Nyau* cult, an important element in the traditional religion of the Cewa peoples. The *Nyau* provoked lesser struggles with the Dutch Reformed and other Protestant missions. Also see M. Schoffeleers, 'The *Nyau* societies: our present understanding', *Society of Malawi Journal*, vol. 29, pt. 1 (Jan. 1976), p. 59-68.

265 **Nyasaland and the millennium.**
George Shepperson. In: *Millennial dreams in action: essays in comparative study*, edited by S. L. Thrupp. The Hague: Mouton, 1962, p. 144-50.

The author makes an unlikely comparison between the lakeside Tonga and the emerging proletariat of 18th century Britain.

266 **The life and letters of Arthur Fraser Sim.**
Arthur Fraser Sim. London: Universities' Mission to
Central Africa, 1901. 3rd ed. 278p.
Sim was an Anglican missionary at Nkhotakota from June 1894 until he died in
October 1895. His letters reveal the difficulties encountered by the early mission-
aries in trying to suppress the slave trade on the lake.

267 **John Cuthbert Smith: 36 years in Nyasaland.**
Compiled by E. H. Smith. London: Priory Press [n.d.].
11p.
Smith was founder of Milolongwe Evangelical Mission near Blantyre.

268 **Dawn in the Dark Continent: Africa and its missions.**
James Stewart. London: Oliphant, Anderson & Ferrier,
1903. 400p.
This book represents the 1902 Duff Missionary Lectures. It covers many Protes-
tant efforts throughout the continent, and chapter 8 is devoted to Blantyre and
Livingstonia Missions. For updates on mission work in Malawi, see William J. W.
Roome, *A great emancipation: a mission survey of Nyasaland Central Africa*
(London: World Dominion Press, 1926); and *Annual reports of the Christian
Service Committee of the churches in Malawi* (Blantyre). The C.S.C. is an
ecumenical group founded by the Revd. Tom Colvin of Blantyre Mission.

269 **The priest from the lakeside.**
John C. Weller. Blantyre, Malawi: Claim, 1971. 69p.
The story of Leonard Kamungu, who was born in 1877 and became an Anglican
missionary in Malawi and Zambia. He died in 1913, but was revered for many
years after by his parishioners and co-workers. For more on Kamungu and his
era, see Bishop J. E. Hine, *Days gone by* (London: John Murray, 1924); and D.
Y. Mills, *An African priest and missionary: being a sketch of the life of Leonard
Mattiya Kamungu, priest of the U.M.C.A.* (London: Universities' Mission to Central Africa, 1914).

270 **Stewart of Lovedale: the life of James Stewart.**
James Wells. London: Hodder & Stoughton, 1909. 419p.
The author writes of Stewart: 'He was a great Christian, but not any conventional type, and he did not employ the conventional language of religion. His
inner life was cultivated with great care, fearing lest his censer should hold old
ashes instead of fresh incense....At the centre of all his activities we find a man
on his knees praying for the consecrated flame and the undivided surrender'.

271 **Some reminiscences of Nyasaland.**
Frank Winspear. *Nyasaland Journal*, vol. 13, pt. 2 (July
1960), p. 35-74.
Canon Winspear arrived in Nyasaland in 1906 and spent the next fifty years on
Likoma Island. This article is devoted to his ministry and the changes he saw in
African culture. Also see his 'A short history of the Universities' Mission', *Nyas-
aland Journal*, vol. 9, pt. 1 (Jan. 1956), p. 11-50.

Religion

272 **Sectarianism in Southern Nyasaland.**
R. L. Wishlade. London, New York: Oxford University Press, 1965. 162p.
The author carried out his research in 1958-60 as a fellow of the International African Institute. He studied over thirty Southern Malawi sects, but concentrated on two, the Ethiopian Church and the Faithful Church of Christ. To differentiate between churches and sects, Wishdale uses the criterion of scale. Most of his sects were what he termed the 'simple secessionist type'; these were formed, not as a result of doctrinal or ritual differences with the home body, but as a result of protests against the organization or individuals within it.

273 **The idea of God in Northern Nyasaland.**
T. Cullen Young. In: *African ideas of God*, edited by Edwin W. Smith. Edinburgh, London: Edinburgh House Press, 1950, p. 36-58.
Although he admits the meagreness of his data, the Revd. Young concludes that in most traditional Malawian religions God and man were never together on earth. He found one instance of this, but 'man's habit of quarrelling and noisiness eventually drove God to seek peace and quiet "up above" whence, try as he may, man has never yet been able to persuade him to return. All that has remained has been a sense of vague community with the Power that once was near at hand but now is distant'. Also see J. A. K. Kandawire, 'Reality and symbolic exchange in African religion', *Malawi Journal of Social Science*, vol. 5 (1976), p. 57-66.

Politics and Christianity in Malawi, 1875-1940: the impact of the Livingstonia Mission in the Northern Province.
See item no. 144.

Underdevelopment in Malawi: the missionary contribution.
See item no. 145.

In the wake of Livingstone and the British administration: some considerations of commerce and Christianity in Malawi.
See item no. 159.

The African - a child or a man: the quarrel between the Blantyre Mission of the Church of Scotland and the British Central Africa administration, 1890-1905.
See item no. 183.

Livingstonia, 1875-1975.
See item no. 196.

Anthropology

274 **The Yaos.**

Yohanna B. Abdallah. London: Cass, 1973. 136p.

A classic ethnographic study, first published by the Nyasaland government in 1919. Oral testimonies about Yao customs, religion, and speech were gathered by the author - a canon of the Universities' Mission to Central Africa - and translated by Protectorate medical officer, Meredith Sanderson. With texts in both English and Yao, this edition contains a useful introduction by Professor E. A. Alpers.

275 **My Ngoni of Nyasaland.**

Y. M. Chibambo. London: Lutterworth Press, 1942. 64p.

The Revd. Chibambo was educated by Livingstonia Mission, and worked for many years in the Ekwendeni area. His manuscript was translated from the Tumbuka by the Revd. Charles Stuart, a co-worker. The book was part of a series of simply written volumes which were intended to interest Africans in the great tribes and personalities of their continent. Also see G. D. Lancaster, 'Tentative chronology of the Ngoni', *Journal of the Royal Anthropological Society* ., vol. 17 (1937); for another Ngoni group see Ian Linden's 'Some oral traditions from the Maseko Ngoni', *Society of Malawi Journal*, vol. 24, pt. 2 (July 1971), p. 61-73.

276 **The Zulu of Nyasaland: their manners and customs.**

Donald Fraser. *Philosophical Society of Glasgow.*

Proceedings (20 Feb. 1901), p. 60-75.

The author refers to the Northern Ngoni as the 'Zulu'. He describes members of early war parties as 'dressing in a frightsome garb of cock feathers, carrying a large shield and two or three stabbing assegais'. Adulterers were put to death, 'harsh and terrible punishments, necessary for rough times'. Polygamy was universal, however, and 'the position of a wife of an aristocrat was one of considerable ease and dignity'.

Anthropology

277 **Notes on fishing and allied industries as practised amongst the Tonga of the West Nyasa District.**

M. C. Hoole. *Nyasaland Journal*, vol. 8, pt. 1 (Jan. 1955), p. 25-38.

Captain Hoole was district resident for West Nyasa in the 1930s and wrote this as an appendix to his 1934 annual report. He describes fish nets and traps used by the Tonga, line fishing, canoes, fish poisons and the *sanjika* fish, which swims up the Ciwandama rapids to spawn.

278 **Mponda mission diary, 1889-1891: daily life in a Machinga village. Parts 1 to 4.**

Edited and translated by Ian Linden. *International Journal of African Historical Studies*, vol. 7, pt. 2 (1974), p. 272-303; vol. 7, pt. 3 (1974), p. 493-515; vol. 7, pt. 4 (1974), p. 688-728; vol. 8, pt. 1 (1975), p. 111-35.

Mponda village was located on the Shire just south of its junction with the lake. The Machinga are a Yao group. The diary was kept mainly by White Father Adolphe Lechaptois, and provides a rare glimpse of day-to-day village life along a major slave route before the trade was suppressed. For another early look at the same group see R. S. Hynde, 'Among the Machinga people', *Scottish Geographical Magazine*, vol. 7 (1891), p. 656-722.

279 **Sorcery in its social setting: a study of the Northern Rhodesia Cewa.**

Maxwell Gay Marwick. Manchester, England: Manchester University Press; Atlantic Highlands, New Jersey: Humanities Press, 1965. 339p.

Although devoted to the Zambian Cewa, this book is included here because of its fascinating subject, and because of the geographical proximity of the Zambian and Malawian Cewa tribes. Also see by the same author, 'African witchcraft and anxiety load', *Theoria: a journal of studies* (1948); 'The sociology of sorcery in a Central African tribe', *African Studies*, vol. 22, pt. 1 (1963); and 'The social context of Cewa witch beliefs', *Africa*, vol. 22 (1952), p. 120-35 and 215-33.

280 **The Yao village: a study in the social structure of a Malawian tribe.**

J. Clyde Mitchell. Manchester, England: Manchester University Press, 1956; Atlantic Highlands, New Jersey: Humanities Press, 1971. 236p.

The result of field research in 1946-49, when the author was a research officer with the Rhodes-Livingstone Institute, and when a remarkable group of anthropologists were associated with the Institute. These included the director Max Gluckman, Elizabeth Colson, J. A. Barnes, and M. G. Marwick. The author, a South African sociologist, worked mainly in Chief Kawinga's area around Domasi, north of Zomba. His particular interests were the political, legal and ritual responsibilities of a village headman. Also see the author's 'The political organization of the Yao in Southern Nyasaland', *African Studies*, vol. 8, pt. 3 (Sept. 1949), p. 141-59.

281 **The AmaCinga Yao.**
W. H. J. Rangeley. *Nyasaland Journal*, vol. 15, pt. 2 (July 1962), p. 40-70.

A selection from the Rangeley Papers held in the Society of Malawi Library. Other posthumous articles from this source are: 'The Ayao', *Nyasaland Journal*, vol. 16, pt. 1 (Jan. 1963); 'The Arabs', *Nyasaland Journal*, vol. 16, pt. 2 (July 1963); 'The earliest inhabitants', *Nyasaland Journal*, vol. 16, pt. 2 (July 1963), p. 35-42; 'The Portuguese', *Nyasaland Journal*, vol. 17, pt. 1 (Jan. 1964), p. 42-71; and 'The Angoni', *Society of Malawi Journal*, vol. 19, pt. 2 (July 1966), p. 62-85.

282 **Children of their fathers: growing up among the Ngoni of Nyasaland.**
Margaret Read. London: Methuen, 1959; New York: Holt, Rinehart & Winston, 1968. 176p.

A discussion of the roles of the home, school and local society in the rearing of Ngoni children. Upon the birth of a child, called 'the new stranger', it is presented to its male kin and the village elders, and then is named by its paternal grandfather. After this, it is placed in a 'carrying skin' made from a goat or small calf. A girl nurse from outside the circle of relatives is chosen to care for the infant, and in addition to mother's milk, babies are given a thin gruel made from millet or maize flour beaten into curds and whey.

283 **The Ngoni of Nyasaland.**
Margaret Read. London, New York: Oxford University Press, 1956. 212p. Reprinted, London: Cass, 1970.

Material for this volume was gathered between 1935 and 1939 in the Ngoni areas of Northern and Central Malawi, especially in Chief Gomani's region. The author describes Ngoni history and politics, social organization, family structure, and the 'ancestor cult'. A glossary of Ngoni terms is included.

284 **The relationship systems of the Wangonde and Wahenga tribes, Nyasaland.**
G. Meredith Sanderson. *Journal of the Royal Anthropological Institute*, vol. 53 (1923), p. 448-59.

Sanderson was a physician who lived in Nyasaland for many years, and became very knowledgeable about traditional medicine. He treated Africans during the sleeping sickness epidemic of 1918, and finally became a recluse, living among the Yao because he believed Europeans had contaminated Africans with their civilization. This is an ethnographic study of familial relationships. Also see 'Some marriage customs of the Wahenga, Nyasaland', *Journal of the Royal African Society*, no. 86, vol. 22 (Jan. 1923), p. 131-8, in which Sanderson points out that the Henga believed contamination resulted from sex during menstruation, and that a husband must never attempt sexual intercourse with his sleeping wife on penalty of being called a wizard.

Anthropology

285 **The use of tail-switches in magic.**
G. Meredith Sanderson. *Nyasaland Journal*, vol. 8, pt. 1 (Jan. 1955), p. 39-56.
Dr. Sanderson wrote this article in the 1920s. Tail-switches were part of the regalia of the master of the Yao initiation ceremony; they were also used in ceremonies which preceded wars to acquire slaves, goods and additional women. The magic powers of these tails were occasionally 'fed' by dipping them in the blood of slain enemies. Also see the author's 'Inyago: the picture models of the Yao initiation ceremonies', *Nyasaland Journal*, vol. 8, pt. 2 (July 1955), p. 36-57.

286 **The Lower Shire Valley: its ecology, population distribution, ethnic divisions and systems of marriage.**
Matthew Schoffeleers. Limbe, Malawi: Montfort Press, 1968. 86p.
Professor Schoffeleers, now teaching in The Hague, has made an immense contribution to the study of Malawi's peoples, their culture and their history. Also see his *Evil spirits and rites of exorcism in the Lower Shire Valley of Malawi* (Limbe: Montfort Press, 1967); 'The meaning and use of the name Malawi in oral traditions and precolonial documents', in: *Malawi: the history of a nation* (q.v.), edited by Bridglal Pachai, p. 91-103; 'Crisis, criticism and critique: an interpretative model of territorial mediumship among the Chewa', *Malawi Journal of Social Science*, vol. 3 (1974), p. 74-80; and 'Towards the identification of a proto-Chewa culture: a preliminary contribution', *Malawi Journal of Social Science*, vol. 2 (1973), p. 47-60.

287 **Myth and reality in Malawi.**
George Shepperson. Evanston, Illinois: Northwestern University Press, 1966. 27p.
The fourth Melville J. Herskovits Memorial Lecture, delivered under the auspices of the Program of African Studies at Northwestern University. The author discusses such historical Malawian myths as the fantasy picture Malawians had of the U.S.A., the 'white men as cannibals' myth, the legend of John Chilembwe, and others.

288 **Notes on the natives of Nyasaland, Northeastern Rhodesia and Portuguese Zambezia, their arts, customs and modes of subsistence.**
C. H. Stigand. *Journal of the Royal Anthropological Institute*, vol. 37 (1907), p. 119-32.
An early Cewa ethnographic study. For information on Mpezeni's Ngoni, see 'Notes on the tribes in the neighbourhood of Fort Manning', *Journal of the Royal Anthropological Institute*, vol. 39 (1909), p. 25-43.

289 **Peoples of the Lake Nyasa region.**
Mary Tew. London, New York: Oxford University Press, 1950. 131p. (Ethnographic Survey of Africa. East Central Africa, pt. 1).
Tew discusses the Yao; Cewa; Tumbuka (who include the Kamanga, Henga, Tonga, Sisya, Hewe, Phoka and Yombe); Ngonde; and Ngoni peoples. For an

early look at the people of one particular area see A. G. D. Hodgson, 'Notes on the Achewa and Angoni of the Dowa District', *Journal of the Royal Anthropological Institute*, vol. 18 (Jan.-June 1933).

290 **The politics of kinship: a study in social manipulation among the lakeside Tonga of Nyasaland.**
Jaap Van Velsen. Manchester, England: Manchester University Press, 1964; Atlantic Highlands, New Jersey: Humanities Press, 1972. 338p.
A study in social anthropology in the Rhodes-Livingstone Institute series of Central African studies. In late 1964, the Institute became the Institute for Social Research of the University of Zambia and it is now called the Institute for African Studies. See also in the history section of this bibliography the author's *Notes on the history of the lakeside Tonga of Nyasaland.*

291 **The natives of British Central Africa.**
Alice Werner. London: Constable, 1906. 303p. Reprinted, New York: Negro Universities Press.
As well as this interesting early ethnographic work, Werner published studies of Bantu linguistics. She includes information on religion and magic, childhood, folk stories and literature, plus such arcane matters as tooth chipping among the Yao and how to catch and cook termites. Also see H. W. Garbutt, 'Native customs in Nyasa (Manganja) Yao (Achawa)', *Proceedings of the Rhodesia Science Association*, vol. 11 (1911), p. 87-96; H. W. Garbutt, 'Witchcraft in Nyasa (Manganja) Yao (Achawa)', *Journal of the Royal Anthropological Institute*, vol. 41 (1911), p. 301-5; and Audrey Lawson, 'An outline of the relationship system of the Nyanja and Yao tribes in South Nyasaland', *African Studies*, vol. 8, pt. 4 (Dec. 1949), p. 180-90.

292 **Notes on the customs and folklore of the Tumbuka-Kamanga peoples.**
T. Cullen Young. Livingstonia, Malawi: The Mission Press, 1931. 284p.
Unlike many of his fellow missionaries, Young did not regard African customs as primitive or coarse. This interesting but obscure book describes the ceremonies surrounding Tumbuka birth, puberty and adolescence, marriage, tabus, religion, justice, and death. It also includes selected fables and proverbs such as: 'Travelling is like dancing, the foot is a pumpkin, the buttock is sloth', which means the energetic man will prosper, the stay-at-home will not.

293 **The 'Henga' people in Northern Nyasaland.**
T. Cullen Young. *Nyasaland Journal*, vol. 5, pt. 1 (Jan. 1952), p. 33-7.
The Henga were the first people Young and his wife worked with in 1904. Also see T. Cullen Young, 'Kinship among the Cewa of Rhodesia and Nyasaland', *African Studies*, vol. 9, pt. 1 (1950); and Saulos Nyirenda, 'History of the Tumbuka-Henga people', translated by T. C. Young, *Bantu Studies*, vol. 5 (1931), p. 1-75.

Anthropology

294 African playtime.
T. Cullen Young, Bennett E. Malekebu. *Nyasaland Journal*, vol. 6, pt. 1 (Jan. 1953), p. 36-44.

A very unusual article adapted from a volume entitled *Makolo athu: our forefathers*, edited by Audrey Lawson and published by the colonial government's department of education. *Makolo athu* is an ethnographic study of the Cewa, and this article concentrates on their traditional amusements, describing their games, songs, dances and music.

295 Our African way of life.
Edited by T. Cullen Young, Hastings Banda. London: Lutterworth Press, 1946. 152p.

Contains the essays, written by three Malawians, which won prizes from the International African Institute in 1943-44. The individuals and their essays are: John Kambalame of Luchenza, 'Our African way of life'; E. P. Chidzalo of Nkhotakota, 'The choice of a wife'; and J. W. M. Chadangalara of Mkhoma, 'Father and son'. Each work is full of information about Cewa customs. Perhaps more interesting is the preface written by the two editors, in which Dr. Banda reveals that it was Cullen Young who barred the 'very youthful pupil-teacher, small also in stature' from an examination in 1915, which resulted in his setting out for Rhodesia and South Africa at the beginning of his long sojourn away from home.

Travel

296 Henry Drummond's visit to Central Africa.
Colin A. Baker. *Society of Malawi Journal*, vol. 23, pt. 1 (Jan. 1970), p. 7-19.

Drummond was a Scot who travelled throughout the country between August 1883 and early 1884. His observations of the 1880s, along with those of Young, Buchanan and Laws, bridge the gap between the more prolific writers of the 1860s - Livingstone, Kirk, Rowley and Stewart - and those of the 1890s, such as Johnston, Maugham and Duff.

297 Rhodesia and Nyasaland journey.
W. T. Blake. London: Travel Book Club, 1960. 256p.

Major Blake motored through the Federation following the declaration of emergency in March 1959. Most of the Nyasaland portion of his book is devoted to conversations between himself and various district commissioners he met during his journey.

298 Ulendo: travels of a naturalist in and out of Africa.
Archie Carr. New York: Alfred A. Knopf, 1964. 265p.

The author, an American biology professor, spent three months in Nyasaland. As he wrote in his preface, 'The book I have written started out to be the story of that trip, a tale of pythons, fly spouts, and our curious man Wilson - of incidents, animals, and people of sorts not prevalent in the spate of books on Africa the past decade has seen'. But over the years Carr's light-hearted personal account changed to include a plea for conserving Africa's wilderness areas.

299 One thousand miles in a *machila*.
Olivia Colville, Arthur Colville. London: Walter Scott Publishing Co., 1911. 311p.

Nothing could be more uncomfortable. A *machila* is a kind of hammock slung on two bamboo poles ten feet long and two-and-a-half inches thick; it is carried on the shoulders of four Africans. Teams of twelve to sixteen averaged fifteen to twenty-five miles a day, but it was a bumpy, jolting, and disagreeable ride, especially in the rain. The author and her husband travelled in this manner from

Travel

Chinde through Nyasaland to Victoria Falls, and then back to Beira via Bulawayo and Salisbury. Included are two chapters by Arthur Colville on his hunting adventures. A similar book is J. du Plessis's *A thousand miles in the heart of Africa* (Edinburgh: Oliphant, Anderson & Ferrier, 1905).

300 **Venturing to the Rhodesias and Nyasaland.**
Ray Dorien. London: Johnson Publications, 1962. 208p.
An informal account of the author's two-week visit to Blantyre, Zomba and Mangochi.

301 **Nyasaland: travel-sketches in our new Protectorate.**
Henry Drummond. London: Hodder & Stoughton, 1890. 119p.
Excerpts from the author's *Tropical Africa* (London: Hodder & Stoughton, 1891), in which he urged H.M. Government to annex Nyasaland before the Portuguese could do so. Also see his biography by George Adam Smith, *The life of Henry Drummond* (London: Hodder & Stoughton, 1899).

302 **Travels and researches among the lakes and mountains of Eastern and Central Africa.**
J. Frederic Elton, edited and compiled by H. B. Cotterill. London: John Murray, 1879. 417p. Reprinted, London: Cass, 1968.
The journal kept by Captain Elton who, as British consul at Mozambique from 1875 to 1877, was ordered to end the slave trade. This proved impossible for a single individual, and Elton died soon after he was appointed. However, the record of his journeys into the lake region remains an important early source. Also see Robert Laws, 'Journey along part of the western side of Lake Nyasa in 1878', *Proceedings of the Royal Geographical Society*, vol. 1 (1879), p. 307; and R. I. Money and S. K. Smith, 'Explorations in the country west of Lake Nyasa', *Geographical Journal*, vol. 10 (1897), p. 146-72.

303 **The lake regions of Central Africa.**
John Geddie. London: Nelson, 1881. 275p.
Most of this book is devoted to the East African lakes, but the last chapter deals with the Shire River and Lake Nyasa. It describes Livingstone's journeys in the area, the slave trade, and Consul Elton's trip through the country in 1877.

304 **From the Cape to Cairo: the first traverse of Africa from north to south.**
Ewart S. Grogan, Arthur H. Sharp. London: Hurst & Blackett, 1890. 377p. Reprinted, Plainview, New York: Books for Libraries, 1972.
From Karonga to Cairo, the authors were accompanied by four lakeside Tongas, who acted as gun bearers. One was a minor chief named Makanjira; another, Chacachabo, died on the return journey.

305 A woman's trek from the Cape to Cairo.

Mary Hall.   London: Methuen, 1907. 424p.

Not to be outdone by Grogan and Sharp, Hall travelled through Nyasaland by *machila*, lake steamer, and on foot. Some of her most useful observations are on the construction of Likoma Cathedral of St. Peter's.

306 The route of Gaspar Bocarro from Tete to Kilwa in 1616.

R. A. Hamilton.   *Nyasaland Journal*, vol. 7, pt. 2 (July 1954), p. 7-14.

The author was a University of London lecturer. Bocarro was reputedly the first European to travel through Southern Malawi. His journey is described in vol. 3 of George M. Theal's *Records of South Eastern Africa* (1899). Hamilton's article is immediately followed by 'Comments' by W. H. J. Rangeley, on p. 15-23.

307 Seven years' travels in the region east of Lake Nyasa.

William P. Johnson.   *Proceedings of the Royal Geographical Society*, vol. 6 (1884), p. 512-33.

The Revd. Johnson was called 'the man who never sits down'. His book describes the geography and the inhabitants of the eastern and southern shores of Lake Malawi. While living among the people, he collected the oral traditions which lend a literary flavour to his scholarly essay.

308 The far interior: a narrative of travel and adventure from the Cape of Good Hope across the Zambezi to the lake regions of Central Africa.

Walter Montagu Kerr.   London: Sampson Low, 1886. 2 vols.

Volume 2 deals with Nyasaland. The author had a difficult journey through Ngoniland and hoped to find relief at the Livingstonia Mission station at Cape Maclear, but when he arrived he found it deserted. After his rescue by an African Lakes Company steamer, he canoed down the Shire, passed through a war between the Massingiri and the Portuguese, and finally arrived at the coast. Also see W. M. Kerr, 'A journey from Capetown overland to Lake Nyassa', *Proceedings of the Royal Geographical Society*, vol. 8, pt. 2 (Feb. 1886), p. 65-87.

309 Nyasaland and African exploration.

Chauncey Maples, D. Kerr Cross, John W. Moir.   *Journal of the Manchester Geographical Society* (1890), p. 287-96.

A record of the speeches presented to a meeting sponsored by the Society, at which each of the three men discussed the part of the country he knew best.

310 A lady's letters from Central Africa.

Jane F. Moir.   Glasgow, Scotland: James Maclehose, 1891. 91p.

Jane Moir was the wife of Frederick Moir, one of the joint managers of the African Lakes Company in the 1880s and 1890s. This volume is an account of a journey she took with her husband in 1890 from Blantyre to Ujiji on Lake

Tanganyika, and then back again. She was the first white woman to travel across that part of Africa.

311 **The high grass trail: being the difficulties and diversions of two; trekking and shooting for sustenance in dense bush across British Central Africa.**
Frank Savile. London: H. F. & G. Witherby, 1924. 255p.
This book tells of the hunting trip made by Savile and his wife through Nyasaland and Northern Rhodesia during the off-season, when the rains have come and the long grass makes big-game hunting difficult and often dangerous.

312 **Venture to the interior.**
Laurens van der Post. London: Hogarth Press, 1952. 254p.
Reprinted, Harmondsworth, England: Penguin, 1971; Westport, Connecticut: Greenwood Press, 1973.
This charming narrative is often one of the first books people read about Malawi. It is purportedly about the author's tramp through the Vipya and Nyika Plateaus, but he takes his time getting there, and spends much of the book describing a climb on Mt. Mulanje.

313 **On a recent sojourn at Lake Nyassa, Central Africa.**
Edward D. Young. *Proceedings of the Royal Geographical Society*, vol. 21 (Feb. 1877), p. 225-46.
A first-hand account of how hundreds of porters (called *tenga-tengas*) carried the dismantled steamship *Ilala* around seventy miles of cataracts on the Shire River, between Katunga and Matope.

The backbone of Africa: a record of travel during the Great War with some suggestions for administrative reform.
See item no. 187.

Fighting the slave hunters in Central Africa: a record of twenty-six years of travel and adventure round the great lakes and of the overthrow of Tip-pu-tib, Rumaliza and other great slave-traders.
See item no. 193.

Nyassa: a journal of adventures.
See item no. 207.

The search after Livingstone.
See item no. 208.

Medicine

314 **Mission hospitals in the Federation. 1: The mission hospital
in Blantyre.**
R. Gwen Dabb. *Central African Journal of Medicine*, vol.
2, pt. 3 (March 1956), p. 124-5.
A brief history of the Blantyre Mission Hospital, which later became Queen
Elizabeth's Hospital.

315 **Deaths among African children.**
R. Gwen Dabb. *Central African Journal of Medicine*, vol.
5, pt. 4 (April 1959), p. 178-80.
A study of 1,500 African women of varying degrees of education, for whom the
infant mortality rate seemed to be between 50 and 60 per cent.

316 **The treatment of hookworm infection with Bephenium
Hydroxynaphthoate.**
James C. Davidson. *Central African Journal of Medicine*,
vol. 8, pt. 7 (July 1962), p. 272.
The author, a doctor at Lilongwe General Hospital, was successful in treating
hookworm with B.H.N., as was his associate at Dowa, Dr. M. G. D. Hurley. See
Hurley's letter of 25 Jan. 1960 to the editor of *Central African Journal of
Medicine* in vol. 6, pt. 2 (Feb. 1960), p. 89.

317 **Health services in a district hospital in Malawi.**
Eric R. de Winter. Assen, Netherlands: Van Gorcum,
1972. 303p.
The author, a Harvard-educated Dutchman, spent four years from 1966 to 1970
at Nkhata Bay District Hospital in Northern Region. This is a study of the ways
community health services can be provided at district level, and includes a
description of the community health project run by de Winter at Nkhata Bay.

Medicine

318 **Malawi leprosy control project.**
B. D. Molesworth. *Society of Malawi Journal*, vol. 21, pt. 1 (Jan. 1968), p. 58-69.

The project, endorsed by the World Health Organization, was located in Southern Region and treated thousands of cases of leprosy, which was quite common at that time. There are a number of leprosariums in Malawi, among them one at Malamulo operated by Seventh Day Adventists, one at Utale, and one at Likwenu.

319 **Filariasis on the north Nyasa Lake shore. Parts I and II.**
R. H. Oram. *Central African Journal of Medicine*, vol. 4, pt. 3 (March 1958), p. 99-103; vol. 6, pt. 4 (April 1960), p. 144-5.

Filariasis is elephantiasis. In Malawi it is found only in the Lower Shire Valley in the southernmost part of the country, and in the Songwe River area at the extreme northern end of the lake bordering on Tanzania.

320 **An analysis of ophthalmic cases in Nyasaland.**
O. S. B. Peacock. *Central African Journal of Medicine*, vol. 5, pt. 7 (July 1959), p. 347-8.

In 1955, the government ophthalmic centre was established in Blantyre. In this article, cases admitted to the centre over a two-year period are analysed on the basis of their important clinical features.

321 **Mission hospitals in the Federation. 2: Medical work of the Dutch Reformed Church Mission, Nyasaland.**
Pauline Pretorious. *Central African Journal of Medicine*, vol. 2, pt. 6 (June 1956), p. 234-6.

When this article was written, the Dutch Reformed Church had eleven mission stations, six of which had hospitals or dispensaries. The main ones were located at Mvera, near Salima, and at Mkhoma in Central Region.

322 **Nursing in Nyasaland.**
Alice Simpkin. London: Universities' Mission to Central Africa [1926]. 64p.

Concerns nursing in the 1920s at Anglican missions on Likoma Island and along the lakeshore. At that time, there were seven hospitals and three dispensaries in the diocese, responsible for treatment of the 268 villages where the mission worked. In 1925, 216,827 people attended the dispensary, and 2,058 patients were treated in the hospital. The staff consisted of two doctors (one a woman), twelve nurses, and twenty-five African attendants.

Lakeside pioneers: socio-medical study of Nyasaland, 1875-1920.
See item no. 116.

Doctor on Lake Nyasa: being the journal and letters of Dr. Wordsworth Poole (1895-1897).
See item no. 174.

Social Change

323 **The effects of labor emigration on rural life in Malawi.**
Robert B. Boeder. *Rural Africana*, no. 20 (Spring 1973),
p. 37-46.
Following Read and Van Velsen, the author concludes that, although traditional
society suffered a great deal in the early days from labour emigration (especially
from the *machona* - lost ones who deserted their families and never returned from
abroad), after the mid-1930s migrant labour agreements with neighbouring territories and contractual agreements with recruiting companies ameliorated the
worst effects by providing free round-trip transportation, compulsory repatriation,
and remittances from wages for support of the family in the homeland.

324 **The response to planned change.**
Alifeyo Chilivumbo. *Society of Malawi Journal*, vol. 22,
pt. 2 (July 1969), p. 38-56.
One of a series of studies of the Lake Chilwa area sponsored by the Leverhulme
Trust Fund, this paper deals with the consequences of introducing a plan to grow
rice in Chief Mwambo's region on the western side of the lake. Changes were
noted in the area's economy, in work patterns, in the concept of land ownership,
in the role of women, inheritance, and the extended family/matrilineage. Also see
the author's 'Social research in Malawi: a review of some methodological problems encountered in the field', *East African Journal of Rural Development*, vol.
3, pt. 2 (1970), p. 81-95.

325 **The Indian minority of Zambia, Rhodesia and Malawi.**
Floyd Dotson, Lilian O. Dotson. New Haven, Connecticut:
Yale University Press, 1968. 444p.
Studies of the Indian population in Central Africa are rare. This excellent book is
described as 'a kind of sociological ethnography of the Indian people of Central
Africa', intended 'primarily as a contribution to the study of power: to the meaning and processes of ethnic domination and subordination'. Indians in Central
Africa are in a similar position to Jews in North Africa, and their anxiety is
exemplified by this quote: 'We Indians here in Central Africa are just like a
drum. The Africans beat on one side until they get tired. And when they have
finished, the Europeans beat on the other'.

Social Change

326 An outline of the social structure of Malemia area.

J. Clyde Mitchell. *Nyasaland Journal*, vol. 4, pt. 2 (July 1951), p. 15-48.

Malemia is near Zomba and was an area chosen by the colonial government for community development. The author provides information on the history of Malemia, its pre- and post-colonial social structure, how the social structure changed through time, and some administrative problems related to it.

327 The money that disappears in the bush.

Reimar Oltmann. *Der Stern* (14 Feb. 1974).

A description of problems encountered by the Malawi Young Pioneers, who tried to act as catalysts for rural change. The M.Y.P. are directly responsible to Dr. Banda, but he has had to restrict their agricultural activities to specially established settlement schemes in remote areas.

328 Migrant labour in Africa and its effects on tribal life.

Margaret Read. *International Labour Review*, vol. 45, pt. 1 (Jan. 1952), p. 605-31.

A pioneering study of migrant labour. Professor Read went to Nyasaland as a result of a recommendation in the seminal 1935 Report of the Committee on Emigrant Labour (Travers-Lacey Report) that more research be done on this subject. She concluded that traditional life was changing, but that labour migration was only one of many factors involved. She found that matrilineal groups did not stand the strain of absent men as well as patrilineal societies, except when favoured with exceptional leaders.

329 Native standards of living and African culture change.

Margaret Read. London, New York: Oxford University Press, 1938. 56p.

A study of the economic life of the central Ngoni peoples of Chief Gomani's area in Dedza and Ncheu Districts. The author examines Ngoni agriculture, cattle raising and markets, and concludes that economic progress and rising standards of living cannot be dissociated from political and social development.

330 Labor migration as a positive factor in the continuity of Tonga tribal society.

Jaap Van Velsen. *Economic Development and Cultural Change*, vol. 8, pt. 3 (April 1960), p. 265-79.

Based on research from 1952 to 1955, the author concludes that, regardless of how long they remained in urban areas, Tongas always maintained their interest in home life because they intended to return. They retained their positions in Tonga society and exerted a conservative influence on it. Increasing urbanization only meant that more Africans remained in towns for longer periods, not that they became permanent urban dwellers.

331 **Training Malawi's youth: the work of the Malawi Young Pioneers.**
A. W. Wood. *Community Development Journal*, vol. 5, pt. 3 (July 1970), p. 130-8.

When he wrote this article, Dr. Wood was the education research officer at the Commonwealth Secretariat in London, with special responsibility for youth, adult education, and community development. The Malawi Young Pioneers established their first youth training course at Nasawa in August 1963, and based the training pattern on that of the Ghana Young Pioneers, the first national youth organization in English-speaking Africa. Soon after, Dr. Banda brought the M.Y.P. under his direct supervision, and asked the Israeli Embassy to provide trainers in rural development. The Young Pioneers participate in land settlement schemes, organize rural youth as well as secondary students, and work closely with the agricultural extension service.

Education

332 **Ecological education and natural resources development.**
Cornell Dudley. *Society of Malawi Journal*, vol. 30, pt. 2
(July 1977), p. 18-25.
The author is an American biologist at the University of Malawi. He argues that,
in spite of the difficulties, Africa must be educated in ecology, the environment
and conservation. Population and technology are increasing, and at the same time
resources are decreasing and ecological knowledge is lacking. Solutions to environ-
mental problems may be unpopular, but are necessary for survival. Also see P. J.
H. Clark, 'Education and environment problems in rural Malawi', *Rural Africana*, no. 21 (1973).

333 **Education's priority is for practical needs not academicians.**
M. M. Lungu. *New Commonwealth*, vol. 49, pt. 3 (March
1970), p. 26-7.
The title of this article also sums up Dr. Banda's educational philosophy. Also see
the author's 'The rapid expansion of education', *New Commonwealth and World
Development*, no. 1 (Jan. 1972), p. 28-9; and 'Education in development: report of
the survey team on education in Malawi', *Minerva*, vol. 3, pt. 2 (Winter 1965), p.
233-44; and T. David Williams, 'Educational development in Malawi: heritage
and prospects', *Africa Today*, vol. 14, pt. 2 (1967), p. 16-18.

334 **Malawi, Libraries in.**
Roderick S. Mabomba. In: *Encyclopedia of Library and
Information Science. Vol. 17.* Edited by A. Kent, H.
Lancour, J. E. Daily. New York: Marcel Dekker, 1976, p.
1-56.
A history and description of all libraries in the country. Also see three articles in
Rhodesian Librarian, vol. 2, pt. 3 (1970): W. J. Plumbe, 'The University of
Malawi library', p. 55-63; A. F. Johnson, 'The Malawi national library service', p.
64-6; and J. D. C. Drew, 'The library of the National Archives of Malawi', p.
74-8.

335 The socio-political significance of educational initiatives in Malawi, 1899-1939.

Roderick J. Macdonald. *Transafrican Journal of History*, vol. 2, pt. 2 (1972), p. 69-93.

'The varied activities of Malawi's numerically small but influential élite contributed substantially to the climate of opinion which, in turn, led to a substantial expansion of social services directed toward the benefit of the people of the country as a whole'.

336 Visit to a new African university.

Roderick J. Macdonald. *African Report* (Feb. 1966), p. 38-40.

Inaugurated on 6 Oct. 1965, the arts and sciences section of the University of Malawi was initially housed in Chichiri Secondary School in Limbe; the education unit was at Soche Hill College, Blantyre; public administration was at Mpemba; and agriculture at Bunda near Lilongwe. Since then, the first three have moved to the University's new home in Zomba. Also see Malcolm N. Lovegrove and Jonathan Daube, 'Towards more effective university selection in Malawi', *Teacher Education in New Countries*, vol. 11, pt. 1 (May 1970), p. 57-62.

337 The University of Livingstonia.

John McCracken. *Society of Malawi Journal*, vol. 27, pt. 2 (July 1974), p. 14-23.

This paper records the ill-fated plans of the 1920s and 1930s to create an African university at Overtoun Institution at Khondowe. Also see Robert Laws, 'Native education in Nyasaland', *Journal of the Africa Society*, vol. 28 (1929), p. 347-67.

338 Directory of Malawi libraries.

S. M. Made, T. M. Brown. Zomba, Malawi: University of Malawi Library, 1976. 112p. (Library Publication, no. 3).

Made is a Zimbabwean and was at one time the head of the university library.

339 Education in East Africa. Chapter 8: Nyasaland.

Phelps-Stokes Commission. In: *Phelps-Stokes Report*. New York: Phelps-Stokes Fund, 1924, p. 193-218.

The Ghanaian James Aggrey was a member of the Phelps-Stokes Commission. Excited Nyasalanders thought he was the forerunner of American blacks who would liberate Africa from servitude to the white race. Other members of the commission were Americans: the educator, Dr. Thomas J. Jones of Columbia University; lawyer James H. Dillard; and agriculturalist Dr. Homer L. Shantz. They concluded that the country had great untapped resources and that the people were not taking full advantage of mission education. A list of recommendations is appended to the report.

Education

340 The story of school education in Malawi for the period 1875 to 1941.
J. L. Pretorious. In: *Malawi past and present: studies in local and regional history* (q.v.), edited by B. Pachai, G. W. Smith, and R. K. Tangri, p. 61-9.

The first school in the country began thus: One day in 1875 at Cape Maclear 'a boy appeared with some men who sought work; the Doctor [Laws] pounced upon him and enrolled him as his first scholar...when the men left the boy went with them, but returned in a fortnight and surprised the Doctor with what he had retained. Presently there were four boys laboriously learning the letters and making progress'.

341 The Ngoni and Western education.
Margaret Read. In: *Colonialism in Africa, 1870-1960. Vol. 3: Profiles of change: African society and colonial rule*, edited by Victor Tumer. London: Cambridge University Press, 1971, p. 346-92.

The author describes three ways in which literacy and school education affected Ngoni life and culture: first by supplying a written history of the Ngoni; second by giving access to employment in Malawi and neighbouring countries; and third by providing the realization that, even in the colonial situation, there was greater freedom in Nyasaland than in South Africa.

342 Education in Malawi.
Brian Rose. In: *Education in Southern Africa*, edited by Brian Rose. London: Collier-Macmillan, 1970, p. 118-42.

This brief rundown on the background and the financing of the Malawi education system contains sections on primary and secondary school teacher supplies and qualifications. Also see 'Aims of education for girls in Nyasaland', *African Women*, vol. 4 (1962), p. 91-2; and 'Girls' education in Nyasaland', *African Women*, vol. 1 (1955), p. 61-3.

Statistics
(Population)

**343 The African population of Malawi: census 1901-1966. Parts
1 and 2.**
Gilroy Coleman. *Society of Malawi Journal*, vol. 27, pt. 1
(Jan. 1974), p. 27-41; vol. 27, pt. 2 (July 1974), p. 36-46.
After remarking on the unreliability of censuses taken during the colonial period,
the author identifies the most important recent population trend as the tremendous increase in the numbers of young children and teenagers. This has grave
implications for the future of the already crowded country. Also see G. Coleman,
*The analysis of internal migration in a less developed country: some preliminary
data considerations with examples from Malawi* (Norwich, England: University
of East Anglia, 1976. (Development Studies Discussion Paper, no. 11)). For
earlier population studies see J. C. Mitchell, 'An estimate of fertility in some Yao
hamlets in Liwonde District of Southern Nyasaland', *Africa*, vol. 19 (Oct. 1949),
p. 293-308; and Guy Atkins, 'The Nyanja-speaking population of Nyasaland and
Northern Rhodesia (a statistical estimate)', *African Studies*, vol 9, pt. 1 (1950),
p. 35-9.

344 Population review 1970: Malawi.
James R. Hooker. *American Universities Field Staff
Reports*, vol. 15, pt. 1 (1971), 8p.
'Malawi's population density is one of the highest in Africa. The government, the
ruling party, and President Banda are all officially opposed to birth control, to
population planning, and the dissemination of information about sex. Current
planning for Malawi's agricultural development calls for a larger, not a stable
population.' Also see J. R. Hooker, 'Malawi', in *Population: perspective, 1971*,
edited by Harrison Brown and Alan Sweezy (San Francisco, California: Freeman,
Cooper, 1972).

Statistics (Population)

345 **Malawi: population census 1966 - final report.**
Zomba, Malawi: National Statistical Office of Malawi,
1971. 49p.

1966 was the first time a systematic effort was made to take a genuine census in
the country. The total population was 4,039,583. Another census was taken in
1976, and some details from it have been published in the *Malawi statistical
yearbook for 1977* (Zomba: National Statistical Office). This numbers the
current population at 5,561,821, of which 43.5 per cent are under the age of 14.
The annual rate of increase over the past decade was 2.9 per cent, one of the
world's highest. For information on an earlier census see S. S. Murray, *Report of
the census of 1926* (Zomba: Government Printer, 1926).

346 **Spatial, demographic, social and economic characteristics of
the population of Malawi, 1966: an analysis of the results of
the 1966 census for information areas of the third and fourth
order.**
G. M. Stubbs.   Blantyre, Malawi: University of Malawi,
Chancellor College, Dept. of Geography, Regional Planning
Group, 1970. v + 81ff.

The third order deals with districts, and the fourth order with chiefs, sub-chiefs
and urban areas. For an earlier attempt at this type of analysis see F. Dixey,
'The distribution of population in Nyasaland', *Geographical Review*, vol. 28
(1928). Also see D. H. Milanzi, *Analysis of Malawian passport applicants
abroad, 1965-67* (Zomba, Malawi: National Statistical Office, 1970. (Research
Paper, no. 19)); and D. G. Bettison, 'The demographic structure of seventeen
villages in the peri-urban area of Blantyre-Limbe, Nyasaland', *Rhodes-
Livingstone Communications*, no. 11 (1958).

Politics

347 Federation in Central Africa.

Hastings K. Banda, Harry Nkumbula. Privately printed, 1949. 26p.

This pamphlet was prompted by a meeting of Europeans at Victoria Falls, 16-17 Feb. 1949, at which the Federation scheme was announced. Twelve days later, Africans from Nyasaland and Northern Rhodesia living in the United Kingdom met and unanimously rejected the plan. The two authors were chosen to state their objections and this pamphlet was the result.

348 Politics in a changing society: a political history of the Fort Jameson Ngoni.

J. A. Barnes. Manchester, England: Manchester University Press; Atlantic Highlands, New Jersey: Humanities Press, 1967. 245p.

Based on twenty months of fieldwork in Northern Rhodesia and Nyasaland during 1946-49 while the author was a Rhodes-Livingstone Institute research officer, this volume covers Paramount Chief Mpezeni Jere's area in western Malawi and eastern Zambia for the period 1821 to 1949. Barnes is a social anthropologist who worked at the same time M. G. Marwick was carrying out his research among the nearby Cewa. Barnes also has a chapter entitled, 'Fort Jameson Ngoni', in Seven tribes of British Central Africa, edited by F. E. Colson and M. Gluckman (London, 1951), p. 194-252; and an article, 'The village headman in British Central Africa: Fort Jameson Ngoni', in Africa, vol. 19 (1949), p. 96-106.

349 Ambiguities in the Malawian political tradition.

Martin L. Chanock. African Affairs, no. 296, vol. 74 (July 1975), p. 326-46.

'The purpose of this article is to look at the ideological formulations which followed the imposition of European political authority over Malawi (Nyasaland) and the cultural and economic changes which accompanied it, and to try to illustrate the growth through time of a Malawian political culture.' The South African-born author, formerly a history lecturer at the University of Malawi, now teaches at La Trobe University in Australia. Also see 'Development and change in the history of Malawi', in *Malawi: the history of a nation* (q.v.), edited by Bridglal Pachai, p. 429-46.

350 **The new men revisited: an essay on the development of political consciousness in colonial Malawi.**
Martin L. Chanock. In: *From Nyasaland to Malawi: studies in colonial history* (q.v.), edited by R. J. Macdonald, p. 234-53.

The bulk of this essay is an account of the Central Province (Universal) Native Association, which is used to illustrate the growth of secular political awareness and anti-colonialism during the 1920s. The author attempts to prove that political consciousness went beyond the élite of pastors, clerks and teachers to include a wider cross-section of the population.

351 **Race and politics: partnership in the Federation of Rhodesia and Nyasaland.**
Edward Clegg. London, New York: Oxford University Press, 1960. 280p. Reprinted, Westport, Connecticut: Greenwood Press, 1975.

From 1951 to 1954, the author worked as a soil scientist in Northern Rhodesia, and he takes most of his examples from there. Upon returning to Britain, he was employed by the Institute of Race Relations in London to write a book about the Federation. He felt it broke up because of 'the incompatibility between "maintaining European standards" and African advancement' and saw the situation in Southern Africa as a 'stark Sophoclean tragedy; the White communities, hemmed ever more tightly into the toe of the continent, will one day stand and fight to defend the countries they have fashioned, to defend their way of life, the existence of a European society on the African continent'.

352 **Dawn in Nyasaland.**
Guy Clutton-Brock. London: Hodder & Stoughton, 1959. 192p.

The Rhodesian author is a well-known liberal who spent many years developing Cold Comfort Farm, a mission-village co-operative east of Salisbury, which was declared illegal in 1971. This volume presents the political views of the then-outlawed Nyasaland African Congress Party, many of whose members were in jail at the time it was published.

353 **Britain's decolonization policy for Africa, 1945-64: Nyasaland, a case in point.**
Peter Dalleo. In: *From Nyasaland to Malawi: studies in colonial history* (q.v.), edited by R. J. Macdonald, p. 282-306.

The author sees the creation of the Federation of Rhodesia and Nyasaland as an abdication by Britain of its responsibilities to its African colonial subjects. Members of the British Labour Party joined with African nationalists to oppose the Federation and its Conservative defenders, and this ensured Malawi's independence.

354 Race and nationalism: the struggle for power in Rhodesia-Nyasaland.
Thomas M. Franck. London: Allen & Unwin; New York: Fordham University Press, 1960. 369p. Reprinted, Westport, Connecticut: Greenwood Press, 1973.

A very detailed study of the Federation, which supports a remark attributed to the first federal prime minister, Godfrey Huggins: 'Partnership of black and white is the partnership between the horse and its rider'. Using data from a survey of attitudes which he conducted, the author shows how the entire federal system was designed to prevent Africans from achieving the goal of 'partnership' between black and white that European politicians claimed was their aim. In fact, they were doing everything possible to avoid it. Nevertheless, the author concludes with a plea to save the Federation for economic reasons.

355 International aid and national decisions: development programs in Malawi, Tanzania and Zambia.
Leon Gordenker. Princeton, New Jersey: Princeton University Press, 1976. 190p.

The author, a professor of politics at Princeton, questions whether there is a reliable process by which international organizations, with their offers of assistance for economic advancement and social change, can exert influence on national decisions.

356 The two nations: aspects of the development of race relations in the Rhodesias and Nyasaland.
Richard Gray. London, New York: Oxford University Press, 1960. 373p. Reprinted, Westport, Connecticut: Greenwood Press, 1974.

This volume was issued under the auspices of the Institute of Race Relations. Mainly, it deals with Southern Rhodesia, and gives an historical explanation of the yawning economic, social, and political gap between black and white in Central Africa from 1918 to the beginning of Federation in 1953. It includes a chapter on land policy by Philip Mason.

357 Dr. Banda's Malawi.
Richard Hodder-Williams. *Journal of Commonwealth and Comparative Politics*, vol. 12, pt. 1 (1974), p. 91-114.

This article begins by asking how Dr. Banda has survived for so long while articulating policies and ideals so markedly different from his immediate neighbours. The author's answer is that he has very firm and constitutionally guaranteed control of all the significant power bases in the country: the National Assembly, Malawi Congress Party, civil service, army, police, university, youth, chiefs, and the women. Following this, the author discusses the internal balance of forces in Malawi. Also see his 'Malawi's decade under Dr. Banda: the revival of politics', *Round Table*, no. 252 (1973), p. 463-70; 'Banda's grip on Malawi', *Swiss Review of World Affairs*, vol. 20, pt. 3 (June 1970), p. 11-13; E. Munger, 'President Kamuzu Banda of Malawi', *American Universities Field Staff Reports*, vol. 13, pt. 1 (Oct. 1969); J. R. Hooker, 'The unpopular art of survival', *American Universities Field Staff Reports*, vol. 14, pt. 1 (Dec. 1970); Z. Nkosi, 'Dr. Banda of Malawi: rogue elephant of Africa', *African Communist*, no. 40 (1970);

Politics

Andrew Ross, 'White Africa's black allies', *New Left Review*, no. 45 (Sept.-Oct. 1967), p. 85-95.

358 Britain and Nyasaland.
Griffith B. Jones. London: Allen & Unwin, 1964. 314p.

Jones was a civil servant in Nyasaland from 1952 until 1961 when he resigned because, as he told an African, 'I serve the Queen; that work is finished now'. During that time he was opposed to the Federation because it was 'a political disaster for the administration...making co-operation with nationalism impossible' but he remained in his job in order to represent the interests of Africans in his district to the government.

359 The politics of partnership.
Patrick Keatley. London: Penguin Books, 1963. 528p.

Probably the best book written about the Federation. It points out the lack of understanding of blacks by whites, and emphasizes the irrational fears of the white population that independence would bring chaos.

360 An election in Nyasaland.
Colin Leys. *Political Studies*, vol. 5 (1957), p. 258-80.

A discussion of the March 1956 elections, in which five supporters of the Nyasaland African Congress party were elected to the Legislative Council by the Provincial Councils. Among them were Henry Chipembere and M. W. Kanyama Chiume, who became ministers in Dr. Banda's first government.

361 A new deal in Central Africa.
Edited by Colin Leys, Cranford Pratt. London: Heinemann; New York: Praeger, 1960. 226p.

Discusses the pros and cons of Federation, with emphasis on the latter. William J. Barber contributes two chapters on the economics of Federation, and Guy Clutton-Brock contributes one describing his arrest and imprisonment. As in most books on this topic, Nyasaland figures only peripherally, but the *Report of the Devlin Commission on the Nyasaland crisis of February-March 1959*, which admitted that Africans in the Protectorate were almost totally against the federal idea, is given some prominence. Also see A. Gray, 'Devlin report', *African Affairs*, vol. 58 (1959), p. 276-9.

362 Bandawe mission station and local politics, 1878-86.
Norman Long. *Rhodes-Livingstone Journal*, no. 32 (1962), p. 1-22.

While he was a Manchester University Commonwealth Scholar, the author made use of unpublished material from the records of Livingstonia Mission to follow Van Velsen in describing the mission 'observation post', established at Bandawe in 1878, and its role in Tonga politics. He found two phases of mission work there: one characterized by active intervention in local politics, the other by neutrality. Afro-Arabs and the Ngoni also influenced local affairs.

363 The Nyasaland elections of 1961.

Lucy Mair. London: Institute of Commonwealth Studies; Atlantic Highlands, New Nersey: Humanities Press, 1962. 87p.

The author was a reader in applied anthropology at the London School of Economics when she wrote this book. In it, she concludes that the election - in which the Malawi Congress Party gained a sweeping victory - provided an occasion for Africans to demonstrate their support for leaders of the independence struggle. A very high percentage of voters turned out, not surprising in view of the novelty of the occasion, both before and since. For more on elections, see J. R. Hooker, 'Malawi's general election (1971)', *American Universities Field Staff Reports*, vol. 15, pt. 5 (1971); H. R. Rowland, 'The Nyasaland general elections, 1964', *Journal of Local Administration Overseas*, vol. 4 (1964), p. 227-40; Bridglal Pachai, 'Malawi's constitutional position and the general election of 1971', *Parliamentarian* (1972).

364 Must Nyasaland be crucified by world ignorance?

Lord Malvern (Sir Godfrey Huggins). *Optima* (Dec. 1959), p. 171-81.

This dramatically titled article by a former federal prime minister argues that Nyasaland was too poor to survive as an independent country. Of its future leader Malvern wrote that 'he was a hysterical character who had intelligence and, undoubtedly, a mesmeric appeal for illiterate people; and that his megalomania boded ill for the country if he ever controlled it'.

365 Year of decision: Rhodesia and Nyasaland in 1960.

Philip Mason. London, New York: Oxford University Press, 1960. 282p.

Mason was director of the Institute of Race Relations in London, under whose auspices this book was written. It is part of a flood of anti-Federation literature that emanated from the Institute between 1958 and 1961.

366 African powder keg: revolt and dissent in six emergent nations.

Ronald Matthews. London: Bodley Head; New York: International Publications Service, 1966. 224p.

Chapter seven deals with Malawi's independence struggle and the cabinet crisis shortly thereafter; the author blames it on the single party system, which he describes as 'seemingly unable to generate peaceful change of leadership without political upheaval and assassination'.

367 Turning point for Banda?

William Ndege. *Africa: an international business, economic and political monthly*, no. 84 (1978), p. 47-51.

Discussion of the release of 2,000 political prisoners, the 1978 elections, and Malawi's excellent annual economic growth rate of six per cent. Includes information on exiled politicians.

Politics

368 Civics for Malawi.
A. M. Nyasulu, D. Potter. Limbe, Malawi: Longman, 1966. 56p.

A secondary school text, written by a former minister of education and a senior education officer.

369 Malawi: between black and white Africa.
Henry Richardson. *Africa Report*, vol. 15, pt. 2 (Feb. 1970), p. 18-21.

The government is the largest employer in Malawi, and continues to import large numbers of British expatriates for key civil service positions, including the five posts administratively closest to the Life President. The government's continuing discrimination against blacks in Malawi and its support for South Africa led the author - a black American law professor at U.C.L.A., seconded by the U.S. State Department as legal adviser to the Malawi government - to write rather dramatically, 'I must confess to a fear for the soul of Malawi'.

370 Nyasaland becomes Malawi: an assessment.
Clyde Sanger. *Africa Report*, vol. 9, pt. 8 (Aug. 1964), p. 8-11.

Describes the poor state of economic development at independence, when forty per cent of the able-bodied males were employed outside the country. Also see Robert I. Rotberg, 'Malawi 1963', *Africa Report*, vol. 8, pt. 1 (Jan. 1963), p. 7-9.

371 The politics of African church separatist movements in British Central Africa, 1892-1916.
George Shepperson. *Africa*, vol. 24, pt. 3 (July 1954), p. 233-46.

One of the author's earliest articles, in which he points out that, although separatist churches caused the colonial government some problems, by 1916 they had 'ceased to act in a genuine revolutionary capacity. Their function had become, perhaps, that of a safety valve'. Also see his 'Ethiopianism and African nationalism', *Phylon*, vol. 14, pt. 1 (1953), p. 9-18.

372 Malawi political systems and the introduction of colonial rule.
Eric Stokes. In: *The Zambesian past: studies in Central African history* (q.v.), edited by E. Stokes and R. Brown, p. 352-75.

A perceptive article, in which the author characterizes British Central Africa before 1891 as an area of *Kleinstaaterei*, where both Africans and Europeans had created their own small, independently governed bases of operation. He is critical of the early administration's 'policy of brusque military pacification', and its 'whirlwind campaign of punitive expeditions'; at the same time, he recognizes that Johnston and Sharpe had a very small military force with which to take on the more numerous and well-armed troops of such foes as the Yao slaver, Makanjira, and the Afro-Arab, Mlozi.

373 **Colonial and settler pressures and the African move to the politics of representation and union in Nyasaland.**
Roger Tangri. *Journal of African History*, vol. 13, pt. 2 (1972), p. 291-304.
An examination of why, in the late 1930s, some Nyasaland Africans began to seek political representation and to create a national political movement. This meant that the previously district-oriented native associations became more centralized at the same time as the government sought greater control over the social and economic development of its African population. Also see R. Tangri, 'Interwar native associations and the formation of the Nyasaland African Congress', *Transafrican Journal of History*, vol. 1, pt. 1 (1971), p. 84-102; Levi Z. Mumba, 'Native associations in Nyasaland', *Zoona* (Blantyre) (24 April 1924).

374 **From the politics of union to mass nationalism: the Nyasaland African Congress, 1944-59.**
Roger Tangri. In: *From Nyasaland to Malawi: studies in colonial history* (q.v.), edited by R. J. Macdonald, p. 254-81.
In 1944, when Levi Mumba delivered his inaugural address at the first Nyasaland African Congress meeting, he demanded political representation, racial equality, and economic and social development, but he failed to mention independence and self-government. This paper describes the ideological development of the Congress over the next fifteen years into a mass nationalist movement seeking political control of the country.

375 **Some early pressure groups in Malawi.**
Jaap Van Velsen. In: *The Zambesian past: studies in Central African history* (q.v.), edited by E. Stokes and R. Brown, p. 376-411.
A pioneering article on voluntary associations in Nyasaland. They began in 1912, with formation of the North Nyasa Native Association by A. Simon Muhango. These groups were the forerunners of nationalist movements, but because they stressed the value of communication with central government through proper channels, they were more rebellious than revolutionary.

376 **Chiefship and politics in the Mlanje District of Southern Nyasaland.**
R. L. Wishlade. *Africa*, vol. 31, pt. 1 (1961), p. 36-45.
An analysis of how conflicts over succession, rights to perform rainmaking rituals, and other traditional activities, were used by local Nyasaland African Congress leaders to embarrass chiefs and gain support for the independence movement.

European resistance to African majority rule in Nyasaland: the Settlers' and Residents' Association of Nyasaland, 1960-63.
See item no. 167.

Banda.
See item no. 191.

Foreign Relations

377 **Malawi and South Africa's co-prosperity sphere.**
Anthony Hughes. In: *Land-locked countries of Africa*,
edited by Zdenek Cervenka. Uppsala, Sweden: Scandinavian
Institute of African Studies, 1973, p. 212-32.
The author, a journalist and former Kenyan government information officer, is
critical of Dr. Banda's close relations with South Africa. He writes: 'The economic benefits to his own country and the token breaches of apartheid he
engineered do not add up to much when compared with the damage done to the
cause of majority rule in the region by his collaboration with South Africa'. Also
see S. W. Speck Jr., 'Malawi and the Southern African complex', in: *Southern
Africa in perspective*, edited by C. P. Potholm and R. Dale (New York, 1972), p.
207-19; D. G. Anglin, 'Zambian versus Malawian approaches to political change
in Southern Africa: 1964-1974', in: *Profiles in self-determination: African
responses to European colonialism in Southern Africa, 1652-present*, edited by D.
Chanaiwa (Northridge: California State University Foundation, 1977), p. 371-
414.

378 **The Malawi-Tanzania boundary dispute.**
James Mayall. *Journal of Modern African Studies*, vol.
11, pt. 4 (1973), p. 611-28.
Since its independence, there has been a permanent strain in relations between
Malawi and its northern neighbour. Differences between the two countries have
focused on their contrasting approaches to white minority régimes, on President
Nyerere's welcome of prominent Malawian political exiles, and on delimitation of
their common boundary along Lake Malawi. This boundary is unusual because
the Anglo-German agreement of 1 July 1890 placed it on the Tanzanian shore-
line; the Tanzanian government claims it should extend to halfway across the
lake, as do most borders of this nature. Also see J. Mayall, 'Malawi's foreign
policy', *World Today*, vol. 26 (1970), p. 435-55. The author is a lecturer in
international relations at the University of London.

379 Malawi foreign policy and development.

Carolyn McMaster. New York: St. Martin's Press;
London: Julian Friedmann, 1974. 246p.

The premise of this book is that, when a state lacks political traditions relevant to
the conduct of foreign policy, then the motivation and perception of the chief
decision-maker become of paramount importance. The author emphasizes Dr.
Banda's background and personality as the prime factor in forging Malawi's close
relations with South Africa.

380 Pioneers in inter-African relations.

Blantyre, Malawi: Blantyre Print, 1970. 18p.

Speeches by Dr. Banda and John Vorster on the occasion of the latter's state visit
to Malawi on 20 May 1970, when the South African leader commented, 'There
are worse places one can be than in Malawi'. A description of Dr. Banda's visit
to the Republic of South Africa is contained in *Bantu*, vol. 18, pt. 11 (Nov.
1971). A very interesting colour film of Dr. Banda's visit was made by the South
African Department of Information, but there are few prints in circulation.

381 The Anglo-Portuguese conflict over the Shire Highlands, 1875-91.

Alan K. Smith. In: *From Nyasaland to Malawi: studies in
colonial history* (q.v.), edited by R. J. Macdonald, p. 44-64.

Forces outside the control of the British and Portuguese governments - the Scots
missionaries and Portuguese colonial officials, explorers, press, and public opinion
- pressed the governments into disputing possession of the Shire Highlands. In
1890, this nearly led to a break in the alliance shared by the two countries since
the 14th century. Also see Revd. Horace Waller, *Great Britain's case against
Portugal* (London, 1890); P. R. Warhurst, *Anglo-Portuguese relations in South
Central Africa, 1890-1900* (London, 1962); P. R. Warhurst, 'Portugal's bid for
Southern Malawi, 1882-1891', in: *Malawi past and present: studies in local and
regional history* (q.v.), edited by Pachai, Smith and Tangri, p. 49-60.

Law and Constitution

382 **Murder and manslaughter in Malawi's traditional courts.**
Paul Brietzke. *Journal of African Law*, vol. 18, pt. 1
(Spring 1974), p. 37-56.

In 1969, Malawi gave extensive criminal jurisdiction to its local or traditional courts, after a European judge ruled that defendants in a sensational 'ritual murder' trial had no case to answer. It was felt this change would make justice more palatable to both the government and the people. But the author argues that resulting gaps between the penal code and customary law, and between the handling of criminal cases by high and traditional courts, constitute a serious legal problem. Also see P. Brietzke, 'Witchcraft and law in Malawi', *East African Law Journal*, vol. 8 (1972); and 'Theft by public servant in Malawi', *Malawi Journal of Social Science*, vol. 1 (1972), p. 65-75; and J. R. Hooker, 'Tradition and traditional courts: Malawi's experiment in law', *American Universities Field Staff Reports*, vol. 15, pt. 3 (1971).

383 **Traditional criminal law in Malawi.**
L. J. Chimango. *Society of Malawi Journal*, vol. 28, pt. 1
(Jan. 1975), p. 25-39.

The author, a government minister, states that traditional criminal law in Malawi is largely a thing of the past. Although punishments such as the death penalty and compensation for wrongs have been retained, mutilation and ordeal by poison are prohibited. He implies, however, that many Malawians still prefer the old ways of dealing with offenders. Also see his 'Traditional law in Malawi today', *Malawi Journal of Social Science*, vol. 1 (1972), p. 42-54; H. W. Garbutt, 'Witchcraft in Nyasa (Manganja) Yao (Achawa)', *Journal of the Anthropological Institute of Great Britain and Ireland*, vol. 41 (1911); G. B. Moggridge, 'The Nyasaland tribes, their customs and their poison ordeal', *Journal of the Anthropological Institute*, vol. 32 (1902); Vern G. Davidson, 'Procedure, the Malawi experiment considered', *East African Law Journal*, vol. 4 (1968); J. O. Ibik, 'Customary law of wrongs and injuries in Malawi', in: *Ideas and procedures in African customary law*, edited by Max Gluckman (London: Oxford University Press, 1969).

384 **Crime and punishment in Northern Malawi.**
   C. J. W. Fleming. *Society of Malawi Journal*, vol. 30, pt.
   1 (Jan. 1977), p. 6-14.

In Northern Malawi, criminal law in its truest form existed within the family circle. When adultery was committed within the family punishment might be lenient, or the persistent offender could be sold into slavery or outlawry. Adultery with a pregnant woman incurred divine punishment. Adultery committed between members of different families was settled by compensation or, if the wrongdoer was caught *in flagrante delicto* he might be killed. Adultery with the wife of a chief was regarded as treason and the wrongdoer's entire family might be executed.

385 **The law of obligations in Northern Malawi. Parts 1, 2 and 3.**
   C. J. W. Fleming. *Society of Malawi Journal*, vol. 27, pt.
   2 (July 1974); vol. 28, pt. 1 (Jan. 1975).

Part 1 discusses contracts, part 2 the law of wrongs, while part 3 deals with paramula offences. The latter refers to cases where no material harm is done, but one party has injured the personal dignity of another, his reputation, or his goods. The difference between a paramula offence and an ordinary wrong is, for example, like the difference between a man's dog micturating on someone as opposed to biting him.

386 **The natural family and the legal family in Northern Malawi.**
   C. J. W. Fleming. *Society of Malawi Journal*, vol. 29, pt.
   2 (July 1976), p. 34-45.

The natural family is defined as father, mother, young children, parents, brothers, sisters, nieces, nephews, remoter relations and in-laws. The legal family consists of one of the parents and his or her children. It may include others, and is an important legal unit in matters concerning marriage and inheritance. Also see the author's 'The matripotestal family in Northern Malawi', *Society of Malawi Journal*, vol. 24, pt. 1 (Jan. 1971), p. 57-63. Matripotestal refers to the power exercised by a matriarch or her blood relatives.

387 **Malawi II: the law of land, succession, moveable property, agreements and civil wrongs.**
   J. O. Ibik. London: Sweet & Maxwell, 1971. 209p.
   (Restatement of African Law Series).

The author is a Nigerian who worked as customary law commissioner for the Malawi government on secondment from his post as research officer at the University of London. Also see Revd. Horace Waller, *The title-deeds to Nyassa-land* (London: William Clowes and Sons, 1887).

388 **Constitutional changes in Malawi, 1891-1965: a brief survey.**
   Z. D. Kadzamira. In: *Malawi past and present: studies in local and regional history* (q.v.), edited by B. Pachai, G. W. Smith and R. K. Tangri, p. 70-6.

In 1891, when British Central Africa became a protectorate, local jurisdiction was exercised under the Africa Order in Council of 1889. New orders were issued in 1907 when the country became Nyasaland. The next major constitutional changes came in 1945 when Africans were first nominated to the Legislative Council, in

Law and Constitution

1956 when Africans were indirectly elected to Legco, and in 1961 when the Lancaster Constitutional Agreement gave the country responsible government. Also see B. Pachai, 'Constitutional progress in Malawi', *Africa Quarterly*, vol. 6, pt. 1 (April-June 1966), p. 4-17. Dr. Kadzamira is vice-principal of Chancellor College and teaches in its history department.

389 Notes on Cewa tribal law.
W. H. J. Rangeley. *Nyasaland Journal*, vol. 1, pt. 3 (Oct. 1948), p. 5-68.

A special issue of the journal devoted entirely to Cewa law, which was especially well developed in such areas as marriage and witchcraft.

390 A comparison of the family law and custom of two matrilineal systems in Nyasaland.
Simon Roberts. *Nyasaland Journal*, vol. 17, pt. 2 (Jan. 1964), p. 24-41.

The two matrilineal systems are those of the Tonga and the Lomwe. The article discusses their marriage customs, how matrimonial disputes are handled, inheritance rights upon death or divorce, and the status of children born both in and out of wedlock. Also see the author's 'Malawi', *Annual Survey of African Law. Vol. 1: 1967* (London: Cass, 1970).

391 Malawi.
Simon Roberts. In: *Judicial and legal systems in Africa*, edited by A. N. Allott. London: Butterworth, 1970. 2nd ed., p. 203-17.

The author was lecturer in law at Mpemba Institute of Administration. This essay is a brief description of the court and legal systems of Malawi. Also see Vern G. Davidson and Colin A. Baker, *The legal system of Malawi* (Charlottesville, Virginia: Michie Company Law Publishers. (Legal Systems of Africa Series)).

392 Legal pluralism in Malawi.
F. von Brenda-Beckman. Munich, Federal Republic of Germany: Weltforum Verlag, 1970. 216p. (IFO-Institut für Wirtschaftsforschung. African Studies, no. 56).

A discussion of the parallel existence of both English and African legal systems in the country.

393 Legal aid services in Malawi.
Bruce P. Wanda. *African Law Studies*, no. 11 (Dec. 1974), p. 37-70.

After studying at the Middle Temple, University of London, and Harvard, the author returned to Malawi to become legal aid counsel and state counsel in the Ministry of Justice, and then lecturer in law at the university. This paper surveys the history of the legal aid programme; the constitutional framework and running of the scheme; administration of the Legal Aid Department; staffing and recruiting of staff; and the types of cases dealt with by the department. Also see the author's 'The impact of English law in Malawi', *Malawi Journal of Social*

Science, vol. 2 (1973), p. 5-20; and N. S. Jere, 'Motor vehicle law and society', *Malawi Journal of Social Science*, vol. 4 (1975), p. 77-100.

Administration and Local Government

394 **Administration of posts and telecommunications, 1881-1974.**
Colin A. Baker. *Society of Malawi Journal*, vol. 29, pt. 2
(July 1976), p. 6-33.

The author became a colonial official after the Second World War, stayed on to help train Malawian administrators at Mpemba Institute of Public Administration, and now lives in Wales. Also see his *Johnston's administration, 1891-1897* (Zomba, Malawi: Government Press, 1971. (Department of Antiquities Publication, no. 9)), which contains a list of officers in the public service during those years; and 'The development of the administration to 1897', in *Malawi: the history of a nation* (q.v.), edited by Bridglal Pachai, p. 323-43.

395 **The administrative service of Malawi: a case study in Africanisation.**
Colin A. Baker. *Journal of Modern African Studies*, vol. 10, pt. 2 (1972), p. 543-60.

One of the reasons for the 1964-65 cabinet crisis soon after independence was Dr. Banda's plan for a slow Africanization of his administration, particularly at policy-making levels. He wanted to be certain he could trust these officials, and so he continued to use expatriates as permanent secretaries, especially in key ministries such as agriculture and natural resources, which are large, technical, and play a vital role in economic development. However, by 1972 eighty-five per cent of the administrative service was Africanized.

396 **An inquiry into the development of native administration in Nyasaland.**
Timothy Kiel Barnekov. Syracuse, New York: Syracuse University. Program of Eastern African Studies, 1967. 129p. (Occasional Paper, no. 48).
The author, a Peace Corps health worker from 1964 to 1966, researched this book in the Zomba Archives.

397 **Local government in Malawi.**
G. L. Cramp, W. J. O. Jeppe. In: *Local government in Southern Africa*, edited by W. B. Vosloo, D. A. Kotze, W. J. O. Jeppe. Pretoria: Academica, 1974, p. 244-70.
Jeppe is senior lecturer in Bantu law and administration at the University of Stellenbosch, and Cramp is chief local government planning officer for the Malawi government. They emphasize the strict control exercised by central government over local authorities, and claim it is necessary because of the shortage of trained officials experienced in local government and because the single party system demands full political control of all aspects of the state. Also see T. D. Thomson, 'Local government training in Nyasaland', *Journal of African Administration*, vol. 8 (1956), p. 196-202; H. G. Graham-Jolly, 'The progress of local government in Nyasaland', *Journal of African Administration*, vol. 7 (1955), p. 188-92.

398 **Local politics and administration during the colonial period in Malawi.**
Z. D. Kadzamira. *Malawi Journal of Social Science*, vol. 3 (1974), p. 5-19.
Deals with the institutional machinery through which participation in local politics was sought, rather than specific issues around which a comprehensive picture of local politics during the colonial period can be drawn. At the beginning of the colonial period, the government's main task was the governing of the diverse inhabitants, rather than the purposeful development of local government structures. During the 1940s, Provincial Councils provided a limited forum for chiefs and their advisers to articulate matters affecting the welfare of Malawians. Chiefs remained in an ambivalent position throughout the colonial period and, after 1961, their role was taken over by the Malawi Congress Party.

399 **District development committees in Malawi: a case study in Africanisation.**
R. A. Miller. *Journal of Administration Overseas*, vol. 9 (1970), p. 129-42.
Points out that the U.S. Peace Corps was asked to leave Malawi partly because of the volunteers' over-enthusiastic determination to make the district development committees - which they co-ordinated - genuine channels for grievances to pass from the village level to the capital.

Administration and Local Government

400 African initiatives in local administration in colonial Malawi: the case of the M'Mbelwa African administrative council of Mzimba District.
Bridglal Pachai. In: *From Nyasaland to Malawi: studies in colonial history* (q.v.), edited by R. J. Macdonald, p. 189-214.
The Northern Ngoni were unique in being allowed to come under colonial administrative control in 1904 partially on their own terms. At that time six of their chiefs agreed to assist the district administrator in return for annual subsidies. This assistance took the form of a court or council, suggested originally by Dr. Laws, which heard local cases and based judgments as much as possible on Ngoni law and custom.

401 Development of rural local government for Nyasaland.
R. W. Robins. *Journal of African Administration*, vol. 13 (1961), p. 148-57.
Robins was a local government officer in the colonial administration, and his paper describes three phases in the development of rural local government. Phase one was prior to 1953, when native authorities exercised jurisdiction over Africans in certain areas; phase two lasted from 1953 to 1960 and was dubbed an 'experiment' in the establishment of district councils; phase three, after 1960, was called 'the new look', and tried to define and separate the functions of the native authorities and district councils.

402 The Nyasaland Legco, 1907-1931.
Peter V. Turner. *Malawi Journal of Social Science*, vol. 4 (1975), p. 5-25.
Aims to show how the Legislative Council came into being in Nyasaland, and to demonstrate the interplay of forces within it by considering some of the issues which were raised.

Economics

403 A key to development in Southern Malawi: the Nkula Falls hydro-electric scheme.
J. Amer, A. MacGregor Hutcheson. *Society of Malawi Journal*, vol. 19, pt. 2 (July 1966), p. 29-51.

Before construction on the hydro-electric scheme began in October 1963, electricity for the country's main urban centres was generated from coal imported from the Wankie Colliery in Southern Rhodesia, and from Mozambique's Moatize Colliery. By July 1966, the first stage of the project was complete at a cost of £2,525,000, most of which came from a Commonwealth Development Corporation loan.

404 Depression and development in Nyasaland, 1929-1939.
Colin A. Baker. *Society of Malawi Journal*, vol. 27, pt. 1 (Jan. 1974), p. 7-26.

'The purpose of this article is twofold. First, it seeks to show how, in the case of Nyasaland, the world depression of the early 1930s proved not incompatible with a considerable degree of local development. Secondly, it seeks to show that the 1929 Colonial Development Act was, in Nyasaland, by no means the white elephant it was in most other territories'.

405 The economy of British Central Africa: a case study of economic development in a dualistic society.
William J. Barber. Stanford, California: Stanford University Press, 1961. 271p.

A landmark volume devoted to Central Africa's dual indigenous and money economies, and the readjustments necessary when the withdrawal of male labour from the indigenous economy results in a decrease in agricultural output. The real wage is the significant factor in the determination of the quantity of wage labour the indigenous economy is prepared to offer. The author suggests that, in Malawi, migrant labour numbers must be stabilized, so that the government can determine its labour pool, and thus avoid the inflated wages and decline in agricultural production which occurred in Zambia.

Economics

406 The social and economic structure of seventeen villages in the peri-urban area of Blantyre-Limbe, Nyasaland.
David G. Bettison. *Rhodes-Livingstone Communications,* no. 12 (1958).

A Rhodes-Livingstone Institute team researched this study in Blantyre and Limbe between 1956 and 1959. Also see A. A. Nyirenda, H. D. Ngwane and D. G. Bettison, 'Markets and price-fixing in Blantyre-Limbe', *Rhodes-Livingstone Communications,* no. 17 (1959).

407 Marketing of food crops in Blantyre, Malawi.
C. P. Brown. *African Social Research,* no. 12 (Dec. 1971), p. 111-28.

A study, conducted in 1969-70, of 1,400 Malawians involved in agricultural marketing. Half of these were farmers, and most of the rest were retailers; all of them had low incomes. Also see 'Possible production effects of the Malawi Farmers' Marketing Board', *Eastern Africa Economic Review* (June 1970).

408 The Central and East African directory.
Bulawayo, Rhodesia: B. & T. Directories.

Lists all businesses, with their addresses, in Rhodesia, Zambia, Malawi, Kenya, Uganda, and Tanzania. Also see Frank E. Read, *Malawi: land of promise* (Blantyre: Department of Information); *Facts from Malawi* (Blantyre: Department of Information); *Opportunities for industry in the Rhodesias and Nyasaland* (Salisbury: Government Printer, 1963); and *Resources and opportunities in the Rhodesias and Nyasaland: a guide to commerce and industry in the territories* (Nairobi: Guides and Handbooks of Africa Publishing Co., 1963). The last two are rather out of date.

409 Africa - what lies ahead.
Dunduzu K. Chisiza. New Delhi: Indian Council for Africa, 1961; New York: African-American Institute, 1962. 64p.

A philosophical blueprint for the political and economic development of independent Africa. Chisiza was secretary-general of the Nyasaland Congress Party, and then parliamentary secretary to the Ministry of Finance before being killed in an automobile accident in September 1962.

410 The economic outlook for Nyasaland.
David T. T. Frost. *Race,* vol. 4, pt. 2 (May 1963).

Frost praises Sir Geoffrey Colby, postwar governor of Nyasaland, for steering the country into a cash economy between 1948 and 1953. During those years, net domestic product rose by over fifty per cent, a figure which was only nearly equalled during the first three years of the Federation.

411 The demand for manpower in Malawi.
Desh Gupta. *Rhodesian Journal of Economics,* vol. 10, pt. 1 (March 1976), p. 1-11.

The author, formerly senior lecturer in economics at the University of Malawi, points out that aggregate employment in the country declined in the pre-independence period from a peak of 163,100 in 1957 to 127,800 in 1964, and then remained about the same for the next three years. He attributes this trend to the overall economic stagnation of the early 1960s, and to the rise in institutional minimum wages, which had an adverse effect, particularly on estate agriculture. By 1973, total employment in Malawi had risen to 215,310. Also see D. Gupta, 'Industrial development in Malawi', *Malawi Journal of Social Science*, vol. 3 (1974), p. 35-47.

412 The economics of federation and dissolution in Central Africa.

Arthur Hazlewood. In: *African integration and disintegration: case histories in economic and political union*, edited by Arthur Hazelwood. London, New York: Oxford University Press, 1967. 414p.

While senior research officer at the Oxford University Institute of Economics and Statistics (OUIES), the author served as an adviser to the Nyasaland government on secession from the Federation. He also wrote an article entitled, 'The Malawi-Rhodesia trade agreement', *OUIES Bulletin* (May 1965), which discusses the terms under which Southern Rhodesian products entered Malawi free of duty and, in return, Malawi received an annual fiscal payment to compensate for loss of customs revenue.

413 Nyasaland: the economics of federation.

Arthur Hazlewood, P. D. Henderson. Oxford, England: Blackwell, 1960. 91p.

On the whole, economic union with the two Rhodesias was bad for Nyasaland; the pace of economic development in the country was slower than it had been before 1953. Increased public expenditure in Nyasaland and money transferred back by migrants abroad helped the economy, but the absence of much of the potential work force was detrimental.

414 Nyasaland Economic Symposium.

P. G. H. Hopkins. *Journal of Modern African Studies*, vol. 1, pt. 1 (March 1963), p. 103-4.

Description of a symposium held in Blantyre in July 1962, at which twenty of the world's foremost experts on economic development discussed the problems facing Africa. It was organized by Dunduzu Chisiza, whose article, 'The outlook for contemporary Africa', appears in the same issue, p. 25-38. Also see *Economic development in Africa*, edited by E. F. Jackson (see below).

415 The balance of payments of Rhodesia and Nyasaland, 1945-1954.

A. G. Irvine. London, New York: Oxford University Press, 1959. 643p.

Maintaining a balance of payments has always been very important to Malawi because international transactions comprise a high proportion of its total economic activity. The author was undersecretary in the federal treasury, and this book represents his University of London Ph.D. thesis. Also see A. S. Silke, *The 1956 income tax legislation in the Federation of Rhodesia and Nyasaland* (Johannesburg: Juta, 1956).

Economics

416 Economic development in Africa.
Edited by E. F. Jackson. Oxford, England: Blackwell;
Clifton, New Jersey: Augustus M. Kelley, 1965. 368p.

The collected papers presented to the Nyasaland Economic Symposium in Blantyre in 1962. Andrew Kamarck, Frederick Harbison and P. G. H. Hopkins were
three of those present. For more on the topic, see J. C. Stone, 'Economic development and political change in Malawi', *Journal of Tropical Geography*, no. 27
(Dec. 1968), p. 59-65; *Report on an economic survey of Nyasaland, 1958-59*
(Jack Report), (Salisbury: Federal Government, 1959); *Nyasaland development
plan, 1962-1965* (Zomba, Malawi: Government Printer).

417 Income distribution and development: Rhodesia and Malawi compared.
Robert A. Jones, Roger J. Robinson. *Rhodesian Journal of
Economics*, vol. 10, pt. 2 (June 1976), p. 91-101.

The authors are lecturers in economics at the University of Rhodesia. Their
hypothesis is that income inequality increases as development progresses; when
development reaches a maximum, then income inequality stabilizes. In Rhodesia
the maximum has been reached, while in Malawi it is still in the future, and
further development can be expected to increase inequality.

418 Malawi, South Africa and the issue of closer economic co-operation.
G. M. E. Leistner. Pretoria: Africa Institute of South
Africa, 1968. 7p. (Occasional Paper, no. 13).

The author, a well-known South African economist, describes pre-independence
Malawi as an 'economic Sleepy Hollow'. But he is very complimentary about its
economic development since 1964. Commenting on the large numbers of Malawians working abroad, he predicts that 'a catastrophic upheaval would probably be
unavoidable if Malawian wage-earners were to be suddenly evicted from nearby
countries'. He concludes by suggesting a Southern African development region led
by the Republic and associated with the European Economic Community.

419 Rural development in Malawi.
Andrew Mercer. *Optima*, vol. 23, pt. 1 (March 1973), p.
6-13.

Optima is a quarterly review published by the Anglo-American Corporation,
DeBeers, and Charter Consolidated. Mercer was programme manager of the
Lilongwe land development project - which the article describes - and a member
of the staff of the agricultural advisory service of the World Bank. The Lilongwe
scheme is of special significance because it treats the overall rural development of
a large and populous area as an essential part of improving agricultural production in that area. The scheme is also important because it attempts to prevent
increased productivity from leading to inequalities in wealth and opportunity. As
the author says, 'Lilongwe is the quiet revolution'. For more on the subject see T.
A. Blinkhorn, 'Lilongwe: a quiet revolution', *Finance and Development*, vol. 8
(1971); Brian Phipps, 'Evaluating development schemes: problems and implications. A Malawi case study', *Development and Change*, vol. 7, pt. 4 (Oct. 1976),
p. 469-84; Carlton L. Wood and Harry J. Robinson, *Rural industry, commerce
and credit in Nyasaland* (Menlo Park, California: Stanford Research Institute,
1963).

420 The international monetary crisis and its implications for Malawi.

Joseph C. Mills. *Society of Malawi Journal*, vol. 25, pt. 1 (Jan. 1972), p. 20-32.

Discusses the international monetary system and how it works; the monetary crisis of the early 1970s and its causes; Malawi's stake; and possible short- and long-term solutions for the system and for Malawi. The author recommends that the kwacha should be slightly devalued, and tied to the U.S. dollar rather than the pound, so it would be more competitive in U.S. and Southern African markets. Also see J. C. Mills, 'Price responses of Malawi smallholder farmers: fast, slow or none?' (Zomba: University of Malawi, 1975. (Department of Economics Occasional Paper, no. 2)).

421 Aid and dependence: British aid to Malawi.

Kathryn Morton. London: Overseas Development Institute, 1975. 150p.

A self-serving book in which the author suggests that, without British aid, Malawi's capacity to develop would have been severely undermined and budget deficit problems would have led to social unrest.

422 Trading with the devil.

Edwin S. Munger. *American Universities Field Staff Reports*, vol. 13, pt. 2 (1969), 17p.

Malawi's landlocked geographic position poses economic and political problems that Dr. Banda has handled in the most pragmatic way possible - by trading with South Africa and Rhodesia. Also see J. R. Hooker, 'The businessman's position: observations on expatriate commerce in Malawi', *American Universities Field Staff Reports*, vol. 15, pt. 4 (1971); *Quarterly Economic Review: Rhodesia, Malawi* (1971-), issued by the Economist Intelligence Unit; *Zambia and Malawi, a survey for businessmen: report of the London Chamber of Commerce selling mission to Zambia and Malawi* (1966); and 'Malawi', in: *Surveys of African economies*, vol. 4 (Washington, D.C.: International Monetary Fund, 1971).

423 Break-up: some economic consequences for the Rhodesias and Nyasaland.

D. S. Pearson, W. L. Taylor. Salisbury: Unitas Press, 1963. 85p. (Phoenix Group Paper, no. 4).

The authors were lecturers in economics at University College in Salisbury and their Phoenix Group was an independent research body composed of professional economists in academic, financial and industrial circles. They conclude that economic development would have been much the same without the Federation as it was with it, and suggest setting up a Common Services Organization based on, and replacing, the defunct East African model.

424 Report on a visit to Malawi: fish processing and preservation.

J. A. Pinegar, I. J. Clucas. London: Tropical Products Institute, 1974. 43p.

A report produced for the Malawi Government Fisheries Department. Also see C. K. R. Bertram, H. J. H. Borley, Ethelwynn Trewavas, *Report on the fish and fisheries of Lake Nyasa* (London: Crown Agents for the Colonies, 1942).

Economics

425 The Shire Valley project.

E. V. Richards. *Nyasaland Journal*, vol. 7, pt. 1 (Jan. 1954), p. 7-18.

Periodic floods, caused by changes in the lake level and blocking of the Shire River, led to development of this project. It entailed regulating the flow of the river, stabilizing the level of the lake, developing hydroelectric power, reclaiming swampland, and irrigating areas above the swamps. The project became the centre of political disputes during the independence struggle, but was completed by the mid-1970s. However, stabilization of the lake level remains a problem. For a criticism of this article see W. A. Maxwell, 'The Shire Valley project', *Nyasaland Journal*, vol. 7, pt. 2 (1954), p. 39-45.

426 The Walker's Ferry scheme.

T. D. Ruxton. *Society of Malawi Journal*, vol. 19, pt. 1 (Jan. 1966), p. 32-48.

This scheme provides water for the municipality of Blantyre-Limbe from Walker's Ferry on the Shire River, twenty-three miles from, and 2,560 feet below, the city. When this article was written the project had only recently been opened, and was supplying 400 tons of water per day.

427 Recent progress in Nyasaland.

Alfred Sharpe. *Journal of the Africa Society*, no. 36, vol. 9 (July 1910), p. 337-48.

A paper on economic development in the Protectorate which was presented at a dinner meeting of the society held on 3 June 1910 at London's Trocadero Restaurant in honour of the author, who had recently retired as Nyasaland's first governor.

428 Malawi looks to the seventies.

Philip Short. *African Development* (Nov. 1969), p. 20-1.

In 1969, Malawi had a sizeable trade deficit, but this was not entirely negative because it reflected the growth of imports needed for expanding industrialization rather than a decline in export trade. The rate of economic growth was around ten per cent annually. Also see 'Focus on Malawi', *New Commonwealth and World Development*, vol. 51, pt. 1 (Jan. 1972), p. 23-44; *Bulletin of the African Institute of South Africa*, vol. 10, pt. 3 (April 1972), a special issue devoted to development in Malawi; and David Humphrey, *Malawi since 1964: economic development, progress and problems* (Zomba: University of Malawi, 1974. (Department of Economics Occasional Paper, no. 4)).

429 Towards financial independence in a developing economy.

R. A. Sowelem. London: Allen & Unwin; Atlantic Highlands, New Jersey: Humanities Press, 1967. 329p.

This study of the establishment of a new central bank and of a London-type money market in a financially externally-dependent economy was written while the author was professor of economics at the University of Leeds. It covers the life of the Bank of Rhodesia and Nyasaland from 1952 to 1963 and complements W. T. Newlyn and D. C. Rowan, *Money and banking in British colonial Africa* (London, New York: Oxford University Press, 1954). Also see James A. Henry, *Sixty years north of the Limpopo* (Salisbury: Rhodesian Printing and Publishing

Co., 1953). It is an account of the coming of Standard Bank to Rhodesia and Nyasaland written by the assistant secretary to its general manager.

430 **The structure and operations of the financial system of Malawi since independence.**
J. J. Stadler. *South African Journal of African Affairs*, vol. 3, pt. 1 (1973), p. 34-44.

This journal is a publication of the African Institute of South Africa and the author is a member of the Department of Economics at the University of Pretoria. In 1971, he was director of research and statistics at the Reserve Bank of Malawi. He praises Malawi's financial structure for its ability to maintain monetary stability and to make progress in mobilizing local savings for financing development, without undue recourse to control measures by the monetary authority.

431 **Economic developments in Malawi since independence.**
Simon Thomas. *Journal of Southern African Studies*, vol. 2, pt. 1 (1974), p. 30-51.

The author notes the scarcity of serious studies of Malawi's social, economic and political development since independence, and then provides an examination and evaluation of the country's domestic economic policies since 1964. He comments on Dr. Banda's economic pragmatism and his disinclination to articulate economic objectives; the progress of development projects at Salima and Lilongwe; land reform and investment priorities; the attempt to balance the national budget; Press Holdings Ltd.; and the effects of Malawi's emphasis on short-term rather than long-term development objectives.

432 **Economic development in Rhodesia and Nyasaland.**
C. H. Thompson, H. W. Woodruff. London: Dennis Dobson, 1954. 205p.

This volume, written on the eve of Federation, was meant to interest businessmen in the new political and economic entity. Three themes are stressed: the need for capital; the need for immigrant (white) skills and experience; and, according to the authors, the need to raise the low productivity of Africans. The authors were both government employees.

433 **The East Central African question.**
Arthur Silva White. *Scottish Geographical Magazine*, vol. 4, pt. 6 (June 1888), p. 298-311.

An early article which discusses the history of commercial development in British Central Africa and the corresponding Portuguese attempts to obstruct development. The author claims that before 1888, £400,000 was spent in the area by such 'civilizing agencies' as the Universities' Mission to Central Africa, the Scottish churches, the African Lakes Company, and the Buchanan Brothers.

434 **African consumers in Nyasaland and Tanganyika.**
F. C. Wright. London: H.M. Stationery Office, 1955. 116p. (Colonial Research Studies, no. 17).

An enquiry conducted in 1952-53 into the distribution and consumption of commodities among Africans in the two territories.

Economics

Nyasaland, the history of its export trade.
See item no. 103.

The history of tea in Nyasaland.
See item no. 118.

Underdevelopment in Malawi: the missionary contribution.
See item no. 145.

After Livingstone: an African trade romance.
See item no. 146.

In the wake of Livingstone and the British administration: some considerations of commerce and Christianity in Malawi.
See item no. 159.

Pre-colonial economic change in Central Malawi.
See item no. 170.

Malawi: a political and economic history.
See item no. 172.

A brief history of the tobacco industry in Nyasaland. Parts I, II, and Additional notes.
See item no. 176.

Land and Labour

435 The private domestic servant of Blantyre-Limbe.
David G. Bettison. *Nyasaland Journal*, vol. 12, pt. 1 (Jan. 1959), p. 36-45.
An analysis of the cash wages, age, duration of employment, and reasons for leaving and dismissal of domestic servants. Also see D. G. Bettison, 'Cash wage and occupational structure in Blantyre-Limbe, Nyasaland', *Rhodes-Livingstone Communications*, no. 9 (1958); Bettison and R. J. Apthorpe, 'Authority and residence in a peri-urban social structure - Ndirande, Nyasaland', *Nyasaland Journal*, vol. 14, pt. 1 (Jan. 1961), p. 7-40; Edson Mpina, 'Malawi special economic survey: the labour problem', *African Development* (Aug. 1971).

436 The role of the Ngoni and Lomwe in the growth of the plantation economy in the Shire Highlands, 1890-1912.
H. H. K. Bhila. *Malawi Journal of Social Science*, vol. 5 (1976), p. 28-43.
The author is a Zimbabwean and a former lecturer in history at the University of Malawi. His topic is one of the major untouched subjects in Malawian land and labour studies. Also see Alifeyo Chilivumbo, 'On labour and Alomwe immigration', *Rural Africana*, no. 24 (Spring 1974), p. 49-58. This was a special issue of *Rural Africana*, edited by R. B. Boeder and devoted to rural labour in Southern Africa.

437 We won't die for fourpence: Malawian labour and the Kariba Dam.
Robert B. Boeder. *Journal of Modern African Studies*, vol. 15, pt. 2 (1977), p. 310-15.
Description of the abysmal working conditions during the construction of Kariba Dam, and of the strike there led by Malawians, which coincided with the declaration of emergency in the Federation in February and March 1959.

Land and Labour

438 Land tenure and problems in Malawi.
W. Chipeta. *Society of Malawi Journal*, vol. 24, pt. 1 (Jan. 1971), p. 25-34.

The author uses the ownership of land, soil, and other gifts of nature to analyse the different classes of land in Malawi, and to explain why rent may be paid on use of land. He also discusses whether current land tenure arrangements are in the best interests of economic development. Also see in the same issue, T. F. Shaxson, 'A register of physical facts about land in Malawi', p. 22-34; Paul Brietzke, 'Rural development and modifications of Malawi's land tenure system', *Rural Africana*, no. 20 (Spring 1973), p. 53-68.

439 The Lower Shire District - notes on land tenure and individual rights.
A. W. R. Duly. *Nyasaland Journal*, vol. 1, pt. 2 (July 1948), p. 11-44.

Duly was a customs officer stationed at Port Herald who died in July 1946 in the *Vipya* disaster, when the ship sank in the lake. He prepared these notes for other officials working in the Lower Shire districts. They contain information on land usage, social organization, individual and chief's rights, inheritance, grazing, and fishing rights among the Sena and Cewa peoples.

440 Migration of African labourers in Rhodesia and Nyasaland.
Michael Gelfand. *Central African Journal of Medicine*, vol. 7, pt. 8 (Aug. 1961), p. 293-300.

Deals with the health of Malawian migrant labourers in Rhodesia from 1906 to 1929. As the average number of workers increased from 17,381 in 1906 to 46,811 in 1929, the death rate per thousand per year declined steadily from 75.94 (1,320 deaths) in 1906 to 21.68 in 1917, when 849 out of 39,158 workers died. In 1918, year of the smallpox epidemic, the rate rose sharply to 113.38 (3,717 deaths out of 32,784 employed) and thereafter it fluctuated between 15.39 (610 out of 39,644) in 1925 and 21.04 (985 deaths out of 46,811) in 1929.

441 Labour legislation in Nyasaland.
International Labour Review, no. 50 (July-Dec. 1944), p. 506, 536.

In March 1944, Nyasaland Legco adopted the Native Labour Ordinance of 1944 which provided for the regulation of labour recruitment and contracts of employment in accordance with international labour conventions on the subject. Also see 'Recruiting policy in Nyasaland', and 'Recruiting and native welfare in Nyasaland', *International Labour Review*, no. 33 (Jan.-June 1936), p. 88-9 and 849-61.

442 Land tenure in Malawi.
H. J. Lamport-Stokes. *Society of Malawi Journal*, vol. 23, pt. 2 (July 1970), p. 59-88.

Attempts to show how land ownership and usage have developed in Malawi, and the connection between the land, the Registry Office, and the surveyor. Also discusses proposals for a new concept of land-holding in rural areas, and ideas for reform of land usage and the administration of land matters.

443 Native labour from Nyasaland. Parts 1 and 2.

Nature, no. 3475, vol. 137 (June 1936), p. 921-6; no. 3498, vol. 138 (Nov. 1936), p. 835.

Comments on the 1935 *Report of the Committee on Migrant Labour (Travers-Lacey Report)* which warned that, unless migration was controlled and counteracted, the economic life of the country would be imperilled, large tracts of land would become unfit for cultivation, immorality and disease would render African workers useless, and they would hate the white administration. Also see G. Coleman, 'International labour migration from Malawi, 1875-1966', *Malawi Journal of Social Science*, vol. 2 (1973), p. 47-60.

444 The road to work: a survey of the influence of transport on migrant labour in Central Africa.

David Niddrie. *Rhodes-Livingstone Journal*, no. 15 (1954), p. 31-42.

A description of the *Ulere* transportation network which was developed to carry migrant workers from Northern Rhodesia and Nyasaland to Southern Rhodesia. Workers were moved by road and rail and at its peak the system handled 13-15,000 men per year. *Ulere* means 'free' in Cewa, but homeward-bound labourers were charged a fee. The South African-born author teaches at the University of Florida at Gainesville.

445 Nyasaland - a very junior partner?

Free Labour World, no. 92 (Feb. 1958), p. 18-23.

An anti-Federation article which claims that its connection with Rhodesia created an internal shortage of labour in Nyasaland. Also see C. H. Millard, 'Nyasaland's great divide', *Free Labour World* (Sept. 1959).

446 Land policies in Malawi: an examination of the colonial legacy.

Bridglal Pachai. *Journal of African History*, vol. 14, pt. 4 (1973), p. 681-98.

The prolific former professor of history at the University of Malawi used records in the Blantyre Lands Office and the National Archives for this study. Questions of land tenure are extremely important for development projects, and the author brings his study up to 1968. For more, see B. Pachai, 'The issue of *thangata* in the history of Nyasaland', *Malawi Journal of Social Science*, vol. 3 (1974), p. 20-34; H. C. Norwood, 'Ndirande, a squatter colony in Malawi', *Town Planning Review*, no. 43 (April 1972); Colin Martin, 'Land registration in Malawi', *Chartered Surveyor* (Feb. 1971); Swanzie Agnew, 'The history of the Nkata family's land in the domain of Nkosi ya Makosi, Edingeni', *Rural Africana*, no. 20 (Spring 1973), p. 47-51; P. F. M. McLoughlin, 'Some aspects of land reorganization in Malawi, 1950-1960', *Ekistics* (Aug. 1967), p. 193-200.

Land and Labour

447 **The Blantyre Mission and the problems of land and labour, 1891-1915.**
Andrew C. Ross. In: *From Nyasaland to Malawi: studies in colonial history* (q.v.), edited by R. J. Macdonald, p. 86-107.
A discussion of Blantyre Mission's ambiguous approach to land and labour problems in Nyasaland. Before 1900 the mission, led by the Revd. D. C. Scott, criticized the plantation system, but after that date its new head, the Revd. Hetherwick, came to accept the colonial pattern of development as long as attempts were made to temper it with social justice. From 1959 to 1961, the author was chaplain of Kanjedza Detention Centre where 1,000 members of the Nyasaland African Congress were detained during the federal emergency. For more on the period, see B. S. Krishnamurthy, 'Economic policy: land and labour in Nyasaland, 1890-1914', in: *Malawi: the history of a nation* (q.v.), edited by B. Pachai; Melvin E. Page, 'Land and labor in Malawi: an overview', *Rural Africana*, no. 20 (Spring 1973), p. 3-9.

448 **The development of labour migration from Nyasaland, 1891-1914.**
F. E. Sanderson. *Journal of African History*, vol. 2 (1961), p. 259-71.
An excellent early article on one of the major themes in Malawi's 20th century history.

449 **From socialization to personal enterprise: a history of the Nomi labor societies in the Nsanje District of Malawi, 1891-1972.**
J. M. Schoffeleers. *Rural Africana*, no. 20 (Spring 1973), p. 11-25.
Nomi labour societies are groups of people - either all male, all female, or mixed - who join together to cultivate gardens, plaster and thatch houses, build and haul canoes. They pool their wages, and the money that is not embezzled is used for a gigantic party at the end of the planting season.

The effects of labor emigration on rural life in Malawi.
See item no. 323.

Migrant labour in Africa and its effects on tribal life.
See item no. 328.

The demand for manpower in Malawi.
See item no. 411.

Preliminary notes on land tenure and agriculture among the Machinga Yao.
See item no. 458.

Agriculture

450 **A major agricultural development in Malawi.**
John Amer, A. MacGregor Hutcheson. *Society of Malawi Journal*, vol. 20, pt. 1 (Jan. 1967), p. 7-34.
Discusses the Nchalo sugar estate, situated thirty miles south of Chikwawa on the west bank of the Shire River. Lonrho Ltd., of London, owns the Sugar Corporation of Malawi (Sucoma) and spent £3 million developing the 12,000-acre estate which employs several thousand Malawians. The scheme derives its electric power from the nearby Nkula Falls. Also see Alan Rake, 'Inner strength of the Malawi economy', *African Development* (Aug. 1971); Mwambo Mwale, 'Smallholder tea projects make excellent progress', *African Development* (May 1972); Edson Mpina, 'Modernised agriculture will provide more jobs', *African Development* (Aug. 1971); H. K. Banda, 'My country's agricultural promise', *African Development* (Aug. 1971).

451 **Notes for an agricultural history of Malawi.**
Martin L. Chanock. *Rural Africana*, no. 20 (Spring 1973), p. 27-35.
Although there was change in Malawian agriculture, especially in the 1950s when political tension focused on problems of land shortage and on the colonial Department of Agriculture's enforcement of unpopular conservation and planting rules, the author sees a fundamental continuity between colonial and independent periods, particularly in the crops grown and the maintenance of the estate system as the bulwark of an export-oriented agricultural economy. Also see M. L. Chanock, 'The political economy of independent agriculture in colonial Malawi: the Great War to the Great Depression', *Malawi Journal of Social Science*, vol. 1 (1972); and 'Agricultural change and continuity in Malawi', in: *The roots of rural poverty in Central and Southern Africa*, edited by R. Palmer and N. Parsons (Berkeley, California: University of California Press, 1977), p. 396-409.

Agriculture

452 The supply responses of African farmers: theory and measurement in Malawi.

Edwin Dean. Amsterdam: North-Holland Publishing Co., 1966. xvi + 174p. (Contributions to Economic Analysis, no. 41).

Also see C. P. Brown, 'Aspects of smallholder decisions regarding the allocation of farm resources in Malawi', *Rhodesian Journal of Economics* (Sept. 1970).

453 Agricultural development in Malawi.

Horst Dequin. Munich, Federal Republic of Germany: Ifo-Institut für Wirtschaftsforschung, Afrika-Studienstelle, 1968. v + 248p.

From 1965 to 1968, the author was a German agricultural development worker in Malawi. His study covers the period 1890-1967. Also see two items by J. Farrington, *Farm surveys in Malawi: the collection and analysis of labour data* (Reading, England: University of Reading, 1975. (Department of Agricultural Economics and Management Development, Study no. 16)); 'Some indications of seasonal labour shortages in Malawian agriculture', *Malawi Journal of Social Science*, vol. 2 (1973), p. 61-75; and J. G. Gordon, 'A model for estimating future agricultural acreage and production in Malawi' (Ashford, Kent: School of Rural Economics and Related Studies, Wye College, 1971).

454 Agricultural change in the Henga Valley.

Ronald F. Gregson. *Society of Malawi Journal*, vol. 23, pt. 2 (July 1970), p. 36-56.

One of the author's many striking observations was that, with large numbers of migrant males away from home, the women adopted a system of crop rotation which made better use of the land than the traditional slash and burn method employed when there was a good supply of male labour.

455 Food without money.

James R. Hooker. *American Universities Field Staff Reports*, vol. 15, pt. 2 (1971), 13p.

'President Banda believes small-holder agricultural development - with human willpower and a modest amount of modern technology - can provide a satisfactory existence for many more people than now live in Malawi. Opening up the Northern Region to new settlement is central to his planning'.

456 The structure of the colonial system as a factor in the underdevelopment of agriculture in colonial Nyasaland.

J. A. K. Kandawire. *Malawi Journal of Social Science*, vol. 4 (1975), p. 35-45.

Analyses and sociologically interprets the institution of *thangata* to show how the system of agricultural estates which developed in the Shire Valley and Highlands during the colonial era produced agricultural underdevelopment. The author is senior lecturer in social anthropology at the University of Malawi.

457 **Agricultural change in Nyasaland: 1945-1960.**
Richard Wildman Kettlewell. Stanford, California:
Stanford University, Food Research Institute, 1965. 57p.
(Studies in Tropical Development).
Reprinted from *Food Research Institute Studies*, vol. 5, pt. 3 (1965). Points out
that during the postwar years the real value of the average African farm income
rose very little. Nyasaland's export economy was too dependent on European
enterprise, and the country's rapidly increasing population threatened to produce
a very serious situation. Basic improvements in the pattern and practice of land
use were desperately needed. Also see R. W. Kettlewell, 'Nyasaland whence and
whither?' *African Affairs*, no. 250, vol. 63 (1965), p. 258-65. The author was
successively director of agriculture, secretary of natural resources, and minister of
lands and surveys in the colonial government.

458 **Preliminary notes on land tenure and agriculture among the
Machinga Yao.**
J. Clyde Mitchell. *Rhodes-Livingstone Journal*, no. 10
(1950), p. 1-13.
The study was conducted north of Kasupe and east of the Shire River. Mitchell
found that security of land tenure for women was greater than for men. Concepts
of purchasing or hiring of land were completely foreign to the Yao, and charging
rent for a garden was unthinkable. One chief commented, 'God made the land
(and therefore owns it). What right have you to sell it?' Also see the author's
'Land tenure and agriculture among the Machinga Yao', *Nyasaland Journal*, vol.
5, pt. 2 (July 1952), p. 18-30.

459 **The Lower Shire Valley of Nyasaland: a changing system of
African agriculture.**
W. B. Morgan. *Geographical Journal*, vol. 119, pt. 4
(1953), p. 459-69.
Analyses the pressure put on the African system of agriculture by the growing
population, and reviews the proposals for agricultural improvement.

460 **Reports on the in-service training in Malawi, 1970.**
Berlin: University of Berlin, Institute for Overseas
Agriculture, 1970. 150p.
The results of a two-week study trip by seventeen German postgraduate agricultu-
ral students. They examined the Lilongwe land development project, cattle
marketing and beef production, Chitedze agricultural research station, the
Kasungu tobacco growers' scheme, the Likangala rice irrigation project, and the
Chikwawa cotton growing scheme.

461 **Agricultural development in the Dedza District of Nyasaland.**
Gerald T. Rimmington. *Nyasaland Journal*, vol. 16, pt. 1
(Jan. 1963), p. 28-48.
Beans, groundnuts, cotton, potatoes, millet and maize were grown in Dedza Dis-
trict. The author criticizes the Africans' tendency to let their villages sprawl over
good agricultural land and overcrowd cattle, goats, sheep and pigs in particular
areas. Rimmington also wrote, 'A new farm in the Dedza District of Nyasaland',
Nyasaland Journal, vol. 16, pt. 2 (July 1963), p. 26-33.

Agriculture

462 Cattle in Malawi's Southern Region.
Robert H. Schmidt. *Society of Malawi Journal*, vol. 22, pt. 2 (July 1969), p. 57-72.

In 1969, there were 78,998 cattle in Southern Region, representing twenty per cent of the national herd and amounting to 6.5 cattle per square mile, one-third less than the average for the entire continent. A milk pasteurization plant was being set up near Blantyre to meet growing nationwide demand. Also see R. H. Schmidt, 'The Chileka dairy farmer', *Society of Malawi Journal*, vol. 23, pt. 1 (Jan. 1970), p. 59-68; and *The Malawian Zebu* (Zomba: Department of Agriculture Extension Aids Branch, 1968).

463 African agriculture in Nyasaland, 1858-1894.
P. T. Terry. *Nyasaland Journal*, vol. 14, pt. 2 (July 1961), p. 27-35.

Mostly quotations from the works of Livingstone, John Buchanan, and Harry Johnston.

464 The rise of the African cotton industry in Nyasaland, 1902-1918.
P. T. Terry. *Nyasaland Journal*, vol. 15, pt. 1 (Jan. 1962).

Information from government sources, especially from reports by J. Stewart McCall, who was director of agriculture at the time. Also see *The tobacco industry of Rhodesia and Nyasaland* (Salisbury: Tobacco Promotion Council).

465 Development of cotton insect control in Malawi.
J. P. Tunstall. *Society of Malawi Journal*, vol. 23, pt. 1 (Jan. 1970), p. 20-9.

Without insect control, yields of seed cotton were low, and averaged only 300-400 lbs. per acre. The principal insect pests were red bollworm, cotton stainer, American bollworm, spiny bollworm, pink bollworm, jassid, aphids, and various leafeaters. When spraying began, yields rose to nearly 1000 lbs. of seed cotton per acre. Also see J. P. Tunstall, 'Pupal development and moth emergence of the red bollworm (*Diparopsis castanea Hmps*) in Malawi and Rhodesia', *Bulletin of Entomological Research*, vol. 58 (1968), p. 233-54.

466 Using workoxen in Malawi.
Lilongwe, Malawi: Ministry of Agriculture and Natural Resources, Extension Aids Branch, 1976. 24p.

Oxen are of great benefit to Malawian farmers. This pamphlet is a guide to help farmers care for, maintain, and use their oxen and implements in the correct way.

467 The physical environment of Northern Nyasaland with special reference to soils and agriculture.
Anthony Young, Peter Brown. Zomba, Malawi: Government Printer, 1962. 107p.

Soil surveys in Nyasaland began in 1938, but the war intervened and this was the first real attempt to assess the agricultural resources of the country and to map their distribution. It formed the basis for cropping programmes, farm planning, and other aspects of agricultural development. The same authors published *The physical environment of Central Malawi with special reference to soils and agriculture* (Zomba: Government Printer). Also see W. J. Badcock, 'Soil conservation in Nyasaland', *Corona*, vol. 1, pt. 8 (1949), p. 15-16.

Transport

468 Malawi's early road system.

Colin A. Baker. *Society of Malawi Journal*, vol. 24, pt. 1 (Jan. 1971), p. 7-21.

Malawi's early road system was created in the 1890s and still forms the basis for communications in the Shire Highlands. Only a few sections of the original system have fallen into disuse, a tribute to the skills of such pioneer road builders as Bertram Sclater and William Fletcher. Also see B. L. Sclater, 'Routes and districts in Southern Nyasaland', *Journal of the Manchester Geographical Society*, vol. 2 (Nov. 1893).

469 The industrial development of Nyasaland.

John Buchanan. *Geographical Journal*, vol. 1 (March 1893), p. 248-53.

The first published plea for a railroad to link Lake Nyasa with the Indian Ocean. The lake level was falling and this caused the Shire and a portion of the Zambezi River to dry up for parts of the year, which cut off the land-locked Protectorate from the outside world.

470 Railway schemes in relation to British Central Africa.

S. H. F. Capenny. *Scottish Geographical Magazine*, vol. 17 (1901), p. 363-77.

Contains a wealth of information about trade during the early days: exports; shipping rates; the main African Lakes Company stations as well as those of the other river trading companies; and names of steamers on the Zambezi and Shire Rivers. Also pleads for a railway to ease and cheapen the shipping situation.

471 Railway development in Malawi: the early years, 1895-1915.

C. A. Crosby. In: *From Nyasaland to Malawi: studies in colonial history* (q.v.), edited by R. J. Macdonald, p. 124-43.

Unlike most railway systems, Malawi's was built from the interior to the coast. The first part of the line was constructed to provide an alternative to transporting goods by human carrier around the Shire River rapids. By the 1930s, the railroad extended from the lake to Beira on the coast of the Indian Ocean.

472 The growth of civil aviation in Nyasaland.

J. A. C. Florence. *Nyasaland Journal*, vol. 11, pt. 2 (July 1958), p. 14-23.

In 1930 commercial aviation came to the country, when Christowitz Air Services Nyasaland Ltd. was formed with two Puss Moths and a Gypsy Moth airplane. Blantyre's Chileka Airport opened in 1933. Soon the Christowitz company became Rhodesia and Nyasaland Airways (RANA) and was later renamed the Central African Airways Corporation.

473 New developments in Malawi's rail and lake services.

A. MacGregor Hutcheson. *Society of Malawi Journal*, vol. 22, pt. 1 (Jan. 1969), p. 32-45.

A new 100-mile rail link-up between Mpimbe, south of Liwonde, and Nova Freixos joins Malawi Railways with the Mozambiquan system, and thus provides the country with another outlet to the sea at Nacala. Also see 'Dr. Banda's railway schemes', *African Development* (Aug. 1969).

474 The growth of the transport network of Malawi.

John Perry. *Society of Malawi Journal*, vol. 22, pt. 2 (July 1969), p. 23-37.

A brief history of transportation in the country. Also see the author's 'Transport developments in Malawi, 1964-74', *Malawi Journal of Social Science*, vol. 3 (1974), p. 48-73; and P. A. Cole-King, 'Transport and communication in Malawi to 1891 with a summary to 1918', in *Malawi: the history of a nation* (q.v.), edited by Bridglal Pachai, p. 70-90.

475 Transport on the River Shire, Nyasaland.

Alfred Sharpe. *Geographical Journal*, vol. 87, pt. 2 (Feb. 1936), p. 140-4.

Published posthumously, this article noted that the Shire River acted as a drain pipe for the lake. When the lake's water level sank lower than the river bed, the exit at Ford Johnston (Mangochi) plugged up with floating vegetation, cabbage weed, reeds and other material blown down the lake. As a result, the lake backed up, eventually forming a body of water 10 feet deep, 30 miles wide and 360 miles long. When this great weight proved too much for the plug to hold, the water burst through, taking everything in its path to the Indian Ocean. This happened in 1946 when a flood destroyed a 400-foot railroad bridge at Chiromo.

476 Some old steamships of Nyasaland.

S. G. Williams. *Nyasaland Journal*, vol. 11, pt. 1 (Jan. 1958), p. 42-56.

The first steamship to sail on Malawian waters was the *MaRobert*, which transported David Livingstone up the Shire to Murchison Falls in 1858. Many other stern-wheelers and side-wheelers, single and twin screw vessels have followed. *Ilala* - the name of Livingstone's deathplace - has been the name of a number of these lake vessels.

Transport

Lake Malawi steamers.
See item no. 6.

The making of an imperial slum: Nyasaland and its railways, 1895-1935.
See item no. 199.

The road to work: a survey of the influence of transport on migrant labour in Central Africa.
See item no. 444.

Languages

477 Suggestions for an amended spelling and word division of Nyanja.
W. Guy Atkins. London: International African Institute, 1950. 19p. (Memorandum, no. 25).

An early attempt to clarify existing rules and usages in Nyanja orthography. The author identifies three dialects of Nyanja: Mang'anja, as spoken in Southern Province; the Cewa of Central Province and Eastern Zambia; and 'Lake' Nyanja, spoken by people living on Likoma Island and along the eastern lake shore. Atkins' system attempts to cover the needs of each dialect.

478 The parts of speech in Nyanja.
W. Guy Atkins. *Nyasaland Journal*, vol. 3, pt. 1 (Jan. 1950), p. 7-58.

The entire issue is devoted to this topic. Atkins was lecturer in eastern Bantu languages at the School of Oriental and African Studies, University of London.

479 Bush roots and Nyanja ideophones.
G. T. Nurse. *Society of Malawi Journal*, vol. 21, pt. 1 (Jan. 1968), p. 50-7.

Examines the idea that the Akafula spoke Khoisan languages and were Bushmen.

480 A short English-Nyanja vocabulary.
Thomas Price. Lusaka: Zambia Publications Bureau, 1957. 127p.

A handy volume for beginners because it is limited to the simplest and most commonly used Cewa words. It has been reprinted several times since 1957 by the National Education Company of Zambia (NECZAM). Also see by the author, 'Nyanja linguistic problems', *Africa*, vol. 13 (1940), p. 125-37; and 'The written representation of inter-vocalic glides in Nyanja', *African Studies*, vol. 3, pt. 2 (1944), p. 89-92.

Languages

481 A Yao grammar.
G. M. Sanderson. London: Society for the Promotion of Christian Knowledge, 1922. 2nd ed. 211p.

First published in 1916, this useful book contains the alphabet and pronunciation of Yao, nouns, pronouns, and verbs, as well as information on forms of address, a Yao-English and English-Yao dictionary, and exercises on knowledge of the language. Also see the author's *A dictionary of the Yao language* (Zomba: Government Printer, 1954); W. H. Whiteley, *A study of Yao sentences* (Oxford: Clarendon Press, 1966); A. Hetherwick, *Introductory handbook and vocabulary of the Yao language* (London: Society for the Promotion of Christian Knowledge, 1889); R. S. Hynde, *Second Yao-English primer* (London: Society for the Promotion of Christian Knowledge, 1894).

482 Dictionary of the Nyanja language.
D. C. Scott. London: Religious Tract Society, 1929. 612p.

Nyanja, or more properly, Cewa, is the major language of Malawi and is also spoken in parts of Mozambique and Zambia. This volume was updated and edited by the Revd. Alexander Hetherwick, who was head of the Church of Scotland's Blantyre Mission for many years. Cewa, like most of the languages of Southern, Central, and Eastern Africa is a Bantu language, part of the Kongo-Kordofanian language family. Scott published his original book, *A cyclopaedic dictionary of the Mang'anja Language*, in 1892. Mang'anja was the form of Cewa spoken in the Lower Shire Valley. Because the book is a Nyanja-English dictionary, it is most useful to Africans who want to learn English. For a Latin-Cewa dictionary, see *Dictionary Cilatini-Cinyanja* (Bembeke: White Fathers, 1933).

483 Collections for a handbook of the Yao language.
Edward Steere. London: Society for the Promotion of Christian Knowledge, 1971. 105p.

'The Yao language is at first particularly puzzling to a foreigner on account of the rapid and even pronunciation and the extraordinary number of euphonic changes.' For another early look at Yao by a Jesuit priest, see J. Torrend, *A comparative grammar of the South-African Bantu languages* (London: Kegan Paul, 1891), p. 15-17.

484 A practical approach to Chinyanja.
T. D. Thomson. Zomba, Malawi: Government Printer, 1955. 63p.

Discusses Nyanja noun classes, verbs and their tenses, use of adjectives, and contains a short English-Nyanja vocabulary. Its predecessors were G. M. Sanderson and W. B. Bithrey, *An introduction to Chinyanja* (London: Oliver and Boyd, 1944); and M. W. Bulley, *A manual of Nyanja as spoken on the shores of Lake Nyasa for the use of beginners* (London: Society for the Promotion of Christian Knowledge, 1925). Its successors are: M. V. B. Mangoche, *A visitor's notebook of Chichewa* (Blantyre, 1969); and *Chinyanja basic course* (Washington, D.C.: U.S. Department of State Foreign Service Institute, 1965).

485 Military Chinyanja with skeleton grammar and vocabularies.

T. D. Thomson. Nairobi: East African Army Education Corps, 1944. 20p.

The author, a major in the Kings African Rifles, produced this pamphlet for use during the Second World War. He thanks Captain Cormack, whose *Notes on Chinyanja as spoken in the K.A.R.* was the basis for this booklet.

486 Tumbuka-Tonga English dictionary.

William Y. Turner. Blantyre, Malawi: Hetherwick Press, 1952. 284p.

The author was a Livingstonia missionary when he compiled this vocabulary of Northern Malawian languages. Tumbuka and Tonga are mutually intelligible; the chief difference between the two is pronunciation. The Tonga speak rapidly, and slur or elide the final syllables of many words; for example, the Tumbuka *kulira*, to cry or weep, becomes *kuliya* in Tonga.

487 The noun classes of Ndali.

Leroy Vail. *Journal of African Languages*, vol. 11, pt. 3 (1974), p. 21-47.

Ndali, also known as Sukwa, is spoken by roughly 100,000 people living in isolated villages on the Malawi-Tanzania border. Ndali nouns may be made to express diminution by adding the prefix *aka* to the noun itself, for example, the word for chicken is *kuku* but a scrawny chicken is *akakuku*.

488 The noun classes of Tumbuka.

Leroy Vail. *African Studies*, vol. 30, pt. 1 (1971), p. 35-59.

Professor Vail is both a historian and a linguist. Tumbuka is spoken by over half a million people in Northern Malawi and Eastern Zambia. Apart from Vail's work on the language, most of the literature was written in the late 19th and early 20th centuries by missionaries. See D. R. Mackenzie, *Notes on Tumbuka syntax* (1911); and three works by W. A. Elmslie, *Notes on the Tumbuka language as spoken in Mombera's country* (Aberdeen, 1891); *Table of concords and paradigm of verbs of the Tumbuka language as spoken in Mombera's country* (Aberdeen, 1891); *An introductory grammar to the Tumbuka language* (Livingstonia, 1913).

489 A grammar of Chichewa: a Bantu language of British Central Africa.

Mark Hanna Watkins. Philadelphia, Pennsylvania: Linguistic Society of America, 1937. 158p.

The late Professor Watkins, who taught anthropology at Howard University for many years, was a black American who received his Ph.D. from the University of Chicago in 1933. The Malawian who served as his 'very excellent informant' was Hastings Banda. Dr. Banda still retains an extremely keen interest in Cewa which, along with English, has been designated Malawi's official language. For an early study by a missionary, see Alexander Riddel, *A grammar of the Chinyanja language as spoken at Lake Nyassa* (Edinburgh: John Maclaren, 1880).

Literature

490 **The rainmaker.**
Steve Chimombo. Limbe, Malawi: Popular Publications, 1978. 51p.

In his introduction to this difficult and demanding play, Matthew Schoffeleers writes that it is 'basically a poetic elaboration of an event which looms large in the oral history of Malawi. The event in question is the rise of a separatist religious cult associated with the prophet-priest M'bona, which split off from an older cult dedicated to the High God Chauta....The story begins at the High God shrine of Msinja which he takes to be the place from where M'bona originated, and it culminates with M'bona's death in the south and his recognition as a powerful guardian spirit....The symbolism of the play is extremely dense'.

491 **Visions and reflections: a collection of poems.**
Frank Chipasula. Lusaka: National Education Company of Zambia, 1972. 51p.

Chipasula is from Northern Malawi and now lives in the U.S.A. The themes of these poems are the struggle for independence, love, life, and death. Although the author claims that 'I am not a poet' and that he only writes his 'thoughts in abbreviated form', the following selection called 'Futility of pursuit' will perhaps argue otherwise: 'A Shadow: / Coming, / Goes. / Forming and emerging; / Melting. / Forming sharp images / Then blurred / Fading and disappearing; / Reappearing, / Forming, / Nothing'.

492 **Nine Malawian plays.**
Edited by James Gibbs. Lilongwe, Malawi: Popular Publications, 1976. 171p.

The first fairly representative collection of African drama on a national scale. It is 'fairly representative' because the contributions reflect theatre traditions developed in the schools, colleges, and the Malawi Broadcasting Company, rather than the traditional theatre exemplified by the *Nyau*. Contributors are James L. Ng'ombe, Joe Mosiwa, Enoch S. T. Mvula, Chris F. Kamlongera, Spencer Chunga, Hodges Likwembe, and Innocent Banda. Their plays have been produced at the Malawian Drama Festival, on radio, by school and amateur groups around the country, and by touring university drama groups.

493 Some riddles of the Nyanja people.

E. Gray. *Bantu Studies*, vol. 13 (1939), p. 251-92.

Contains 123 riddles collected between 1930 and 1939 in the Ncheu and Zomba districts. Also see E. Gray, 'Some proverbs of the Nyanja people', *African Studies*, vol. 3, pt. 3 (Sept. 1944), p. 101-28; and R. S. Rattray, *Some folk-lore stories and songs in Chinyanja* (London: Society for the Promotion of Christian Knowledge, 1907).

494 Chinyanja proverbs.

Translated and annotated by William P. Johnson. Cardiff, Wales: Smith Brothers, 1922. 26p.

This is a delightful collection of 101 proverbs. Among them: 'How can you swallow before you have bitten?' An old man quoted this when he was pressed by the author to explain what he meant before the author had thought about what had been said.

495 No easy task.

Aubrey Kachingwe. London: Heinemann; Atlantic Highlands, New Jersey: Humanities Press, 1966. 233p.

An unkind reviewer once wrote: 'Reading *No easy task* is no easy task'. The author worked as a newspaperman and news broadcaster in the U.K., East and West Africa, as well as in his home country. His novel takes place during the struggle for independence, and centres around the relationship between a young newspaperman and his father, a quiet village pastor who is suddenly transformed into the passionate leader of the fight for self-government.

496 Jingala.

Legson Kayira. London: Longman, 1969. 160p.

A novel of village life and the conflicts between the fifty-five-year-old widower, Jingala, and his son, Gregory, who wants to be a priest; the young women Liz and Belita, who have been chosen as wives for Jingala and Gregory; and a number of men who have been working in South African mines. The attitudes and experiences of the miners make them a veritable *Lumpenproletariat*. Also see L. Kayira, *I will try* (London: Longman, 1966), the story of the author's overland trek to Khartoum and then to the U.S.A. in search of a college education.

497 Katakala.

Michael Kittermaster. London: Constable, 1957. 212p.

This novel and another entitled *District officer* (London: Constable, 1957), are both set in colonial Malawi. They are sympathetic to the Africans, although the heroes are romantic young district commissioners. The author was the son of Harold Kittermaster, governor of Nyasaland in the 1930s, and was himself employed by the colonial administration.

498 Mau: 39 Poems from Malawi.

Blantyre, Malawi: Hetherwick Press, 1971. 36p.

This is a fine collection of poems by such authors as Lan White, Stocker O. Hara, and the two poets, Nellie Chirwa and Josephine Kaphwiyo. The following is an excerpt from one of Kaphwiyo's works, 'A witch's song': 'Are you still ignorant / That in the deadliest of night / I have shrieked with the owl / When

Literature

you have in fear / Remained, pasting / Your sweat-sticky bodies to your stinking mats?'.

499 Some Nyasaland folk-lore tales.
M. Metcalfe. *Nyasaland Journal*, vol. 7, pt. 2 (July 1954), p. 46-9.

Five very entertaining tales told by the Yao, Ngoni and Cewa.

500 No bride price.
David Rubadiri. Nairobi: East Africa Publishing House, 1967. 180p.

The story of a civil servant who beds a number of women and is caught accepting a bribe. The author was Malawi's first ambassador to the U.N. and has taught at Makerere and the University of Nairobi.

501 Tumbuka proverbs.
G. M. Sanderson. *Nyasaland Journal*, vol. 5, pt. 1 (Jan. 1952), p. 38-54.

Two examples are: 'Can one lip take meat from a lion?', which means that a minority can never prevail, and 'The ant sent the elephant (on an errand)', which is an apology used when asking a favour of an elder.

502 The literature of British Central Africa: a review article.
George Shepperson. *Rhodes-Livingstone Journal*, no. 23 (1958), p. 12-46.

The author identifies four divisions in the literature of British Central Africa: traditional literature; travel and adventure books written mainly by Europeans up to the mid-1890s; literature up to the Second World War; and the more scholarly studies of the postwar period.

503 The obsequies of Lance-Corporal Amidu - a short story.
George Shepperson. *Phylon*, vol. 12, pt. 1 (1951).

During the Second World War, Professor Shepperson served as a noncommissioned officer with the King's African Rifles. This is a sentimental tribute to one of his comrades. Over 20,000 Malawians were in military service from 1939 to 1945 as infantrymen, drivers, signallers, clerks and chaplains. Six hundred were noncombatant members of the Union of South Africa Native Military Corps, and a number saw action with the 7th Battalion of the Northern Rhodesian Regiment.

504 Tales of old Malawi.
E. Singano, A. A. Roscoe. Limbe, Malawi: Popular Publications, 1974. 72p.

This slim volume contains fifteen tales, among them 'Why the frog croaks' and 'A woman who loved her husband'. Singano did the illustrations and Roscoe, professor of English at the University of Malawi, did the collecting and editing, and wrote the foreword. He has also written *Uhuru's fire: African literature east to south* (Cambridge: Cambridge University Press, 1977), which contains a general discussion of Malawi's literature. Also see T. C. Young, 'Some proverbs of the

Tumbuka-Nkamanga peoples of the Northern Province of Nyasaland', *Africa*, vol. 4 (1931), p. 343-51; W. P. Young, *The rabbit and the baboons and other tales from Northern Nyasaland* (London: Sheldon Press, 1933).

505 **Night of darkness and other stories.**
   Paul Zeleza.   Limbe, Malawi: Popular Publications, 1976.
   217p.

A collection of twenty-two stories dealing with social problems, conflicts between the individual and society, philosophy, psychology and comedy. In addition to short stories, the author has written plays for the Malawi Broadcasting Company, poems, and in 1974 he won first prize in the tenth anniversary of independence essay competition. Born in 1955 of Malawian parents living in Rhodesia, he is presently studying abroad.

Art, Music and Dance

506 **Masks of Malawi.**
   Barbara Blackmun, Matthew Schoffeleers.   *African Arts*
   (Summer 1972), p. 36-41, 69.

Contains descriptions and comments on the significance of *Nyau* masks and dance costumes, and includes black and white, and colour photographs. The author remarks, 'Like Dogon masks, their expressiveness stems from their energetic and direct approach to sculptural form, rather than from refinement of detail'.

507 *Vimbuza* **and** *mashawe*: **a mystic therapy.**
   Alifeyo Chilivumbo.   *African Music Society Journal*, vol. 5
   (1972), p. 6-9.

Vimbuza - or *mashawe* - refers to both a dance and an illness. The dance is therapy for the illness, which is caused by serious social problems with one's family or friends, and is expressed in hallucinations and other disorientation. The dance is performed at night to drum accompaniment and the participants, both men and women, dress in special costumes made from feathers, hairy animal skins and beads. They wear bells around their ankles, and carry axes and fly whisks. The dance reaches a climax with the drinking of fresh chicken, goat or cow blood. For a description of *chiwoda*, a women's dance, see 'Malawi's lively art form', *Africa Report*, vol. 16, pt. 7 (Oct. 1971), p. 16-18. The author is head of the Department of Social Development Studies at the University of Zambia.

508 **Ethno-musicological research in southern parts of Malawi.**
   Gerhard Kubik.   *Society of Malawi Journal*, vol. 21, pt. 1
   (Jan. 1968), p. 20-32.

The author's research group set out to make a complete survey of Malawi's traditional music through recordings, films, and analysis. In Southern Malawi they found various kinds of xylophones, tuned drums (drum chimes), stringed instruments, and lamellophones (finger pianos).

509 The Kachamba brothers' band: a study of neo-traditional music in Malawi.
Gerhard Kubik. Lusaka: University of Zambia Institute for African Studies, 1974, 75p. (Zambian Papers, no. 9).

Daniel and Donald Kachamba, on guitar and flute, formed the core of the band, which played *kwela* or South African penny whistle music, and toured East Africa and Europe in 1972. Kubik, a German musicologist, joined them from time to time as a vocalist and rattle player.

510 The *Kalela* dance.
J. Clyde Mitchell. Manchester, England: Manchester University Press, 1956. 52p.

Kalela dance was related to *mbeni* dance, which was performed in Northern Nyasaland as a pantomime or sarcastic comment on the social mores of the local white population. Also see T. O. Ranger, *Dance and society in Eastern Africa, 1890-1970* (Berkeley: University of California Press, 1975).

511 Nyasaland numbers.
Robert H. Napier. Blantyre, Malawi: Blantyre Mission Press, 1916. 28p.

Twenty-two songs sung by the King's African Rifles during the East Africa campaign.

512 Popular songs and national identity in Malawi.
G. T. Nurse. *African Music*, vol. 3, pt. 3 (1964), p. 101-6.

Also see the author's 'Ideophonic aspects of some Nyanja drum names', *African Music*, vol. 4, pt. 2 (1968); E. T. Chakanza, 'Nyasa folk songs', *African Affairs*, vol. 49 (1950), p. 158-61; E. Kidney, 'Native songs from Nyasaland', *Journal of the Africa Society*, vol. 20 (1921), p. 116-26; M. Read, 'Songs of the Ngoni people', *Bantu Studies*, vol. 11 (1937), p. 1-35.

513 Tunes from Nyasaland.
Compiled by H. M. Taylor. Livingstonia, Malawi: Livingstonia Mission, 1959. 36p.

Words and music for thirty-two hymns, originally composed by Malawians in the Ngoni and Tumbuka languages. They were meant for unaccompanied congregational singing led by a precentor. Among the composers are Jonathan Chirwa, Peter Thole, Charles Chinula and Mawelera Tembo.

Malawi's culture in the national integration.
See item no. 4.

Nyau in Kotakota District. Parts I and II.
See item no. 179.

African playtime.
See item no. 294.

Newspapers, Magazines, and Periodicals

514 The African.
Lilongwe, Malawi: Likuni Press, 1950-, fortnightly.
Published in English, Nyanja, and Tumbuka by the White Fathers.

515 Aurora: a Journal of missionary news and Christian work.
Livingstonia, Malawi, 1897-1903, bimonthly.
This is a vital source for impressions of life in Northern Malawi at the turn of the century. It was replaced by *Livingstonia News*.

516 Bantu Wisdom Magazine.
Kachebere.
A literary publication of the African Way of Life Club of Kachebere Roman Catholic Seminary.

517 Biology Teacher of Malawi Newsletter.
Zomba, Malawi: University of Malawi. Chancellor College, Junior Biology Study Group, irregular.
Reported to have now ceased publication.

518 Central African Planter.
Zomba, Malawi, 1895-97.
This was the first newspaper in the country, founded in 1895 by Robert Spence Hynde, a coffee and tobacco planter. In 1897 it gave way to the more ambitious *Central African Times*, which appeared fortnightly, and was initially priced at 1s.

Newspapers, Magazines, and Periodicals

6d., but soon reduced to 6d. In the latter part of 1908, this publication was suspended temporarily, but on 7 January 1909, it reappeared as the *Nyasaland Times*. It was eventually purchased by a Rhodesian chain, and had a final change of name in 1964 when it became the *Malawi Times*. The official organ of the Malawi Congress Party is the *Malawi News*. See Peter Edwards, 'Press purge in Malawi', *Index of Censorship*, vol. 2, pt. 4 (Winter 1973), p. 53-7.

519 Ecclesia.
Fort Johnston and Likwenu, Malawi: Church of the Province of Central Africa, 1962-, monthly.
A publication of the Anglican diocese of Malawi which contains local gossip. Also see *Nyasaland Diocesan Chronicle*.

520 Expression.
Limbe, Malawi: University of Malawi, 1969-71, annual.
A literary publication of the University of Malawi English Department. Also see *Expression Supplement*.

521 Jacaranda.
Limbe, Malawi: Soche Hill College, 1966-, annual.
Published by students of Soche Hill Teachers Training College. Also see *Soche Cedar*.

522 Kalulu.
Limbe.
A bulletin of Malawian oral literature and cultural studies, edited by Jack Mapanje and Enoch T. Mvula, lecturers in English and Cewa at the University of Malawi. This journal is unique, because it combines contributions from several disciplines in order to develop a corpus of material on Malawian oral literature. It contains articles such as: 'Folk story analysis: basic approaches', Steve Chimombo; 'Oral historical research in Malawi: a review of contemporary methodology and projects', Kings Phiri; 'The trial scene in *Sewero la mlandu wa Nkhanga*', L. J. Chimango; and a long appendix of Malawian riddles. In later issues, more appendices are promised, containing songs, prayers, folk stories, legends, proverbs, myths, tongue-twisters, puns, and poems.

523 Kwacha.
Blantyre, Malawi, 1955-56, monthly.
Newsletter of the Nyasaland African Congress Party; the first issue appeared on 26 January 1955.

524 Life and Work in British Central Africa.
Blantyre, Malawi: Mission of Church of Scotland, 1888-1919, monthly.
Journal of the Blantyre Mission from 1888 to 1919.

Newspapers, Magazines, and Periodicals

525 Link.
Mzuzu.
Published by the Catholic Diocese of Mzuzu.

526 Mala Bulletin.
Malawi Library Association, 1978-
The journal of the Malawi Library Association, edited by national archivist, Steve S. Mwiyeriwa. Vol. 1, pt. 1 (1978) contains: Steve S. Mwiyeriwa, 'History of the Malawi Library Association', and Philip Sewell, 'NATIS, a national information system for Malawi'.

527 Malawi Government Gazette.
Zomba, 1966-
The official government publication for all notices and ordinances. Preceded by the *British Central Africa Government Gazette and the Nyasaland Government Gazette*. Also see Colonial Office, *Nyasaland Annual Reports* for a wealth of information about the country; Malawi's *Hansard*, the official record of parliamentary proceedings; *Proceedings of District and Regional Councils*; and, *Report of the Proceedings of the Legislative Council of Nyasaland*; plus annual reports of the various ministries.

528 Malawi Science Teacher.
Limbe, Malawi: Science Teachers' Association of Malawi, 1965-, irregular.
Also see *Malawi Journal of Science*; *Bunda College of Agriculture Research Bulletin*; and *Weed Seed*, a students' newsletter for Bunda College of Agriculture.

529 Moni.
Limbe, Malawi: Popular Publications, 1964-, monthly.
A popular magazine with a Catholic slant, in English and Cewa.

530 Ntendere pa Nchito: the Workers' News Bulletin.
Blantyre, Malawi: Nyasaland Trades Union Congress.
An English publication of the Nyasaland Trades Union Congress, edited by Aleke Banda. During the independence struggle, *The Worker (Wa Nchito)* was published by the Commercial and General Workers Union. A similar publication was *Umodzi pa Nchito*, published by the National Council of Labour.

531 Nyalugwe.
Blantyre, Malawi: Nyasaland Police, 1951-52, quarterly.
Quarterly magazine for African members of the Nyasaland Police Force, which first appeared in September 1951.

532 **Nyasaland Agricultural Quarterly Journal.**
Blantyre, Malawi: Department of Agriculture, 1941-52,
quarterly.
Began publication in January 1941, after absorbing *Nyasaland Tea Association Quarterly Journal* (1936-40), 5 vols. Also see *Nyasaland Farmer and Forester*, beginning from April 1953.

533 **Nyasaland Journal.**
Blantyre, Malawi: Nyasaland Society, 1948-65, biannual.
A publication of the Nyasaland Society, which was formed in May 1946 largely through the initiative of G. W. Nye, the director of agriculture at that time. At the beginning, the journal was subsidized by the colonial government. The stated purpose of the journal was 'to promote interest in literary, historical and scientific matters among individuals of all races in the Protectorate and to discuss and place on record fact and information about it and its people'. The journal has always welcomed a wide range of articles but has steered clear of controversy. After independence it became the *Society of Malawi Journal*.

534 **Occasional Paper for Nyasaland.**
Likoma Island, Malawi: Universities' Mission to Central
Africa Press, Feb. and May 1893.
This soon became *Nyasa News*, then *Likoma Diocesan Quarterly Paper*, and finally *Nyasaland Diocesan Quarterly Paper*. These papers contained reports from mission stations, lake news, poetry, editorials and articles by leading churchmen and administrators. At the UMCA's London headquarters the mission published *Central Africa* for adults and *African Tidings* for children.

535 **Odi.**
Limbe, Malawi: University of Malawi, 1972-, quarterly.
A journal of Malawian writing from the Writers Group of the University of Malawi. It is a bilingual publication in English and Cewa, and contains poems, short stories, book reviews and plays by David Kerr, Scopas Gorinwa, Innocent Banda, Steve Chimombo, Frank Chipasula, James Gibbs, Adrian Roscoe, Geoff Mwanja, and others.

536 **Outlooklookout.**
Blantyre.
A bulletin of language, literature, and culture, edited by Steve Chimombo. He wrote '*Lookout* is the vantage point from which we can scan the field of what we are doing, and share what we see...*Outlook* is the forum where our view of what's being done can be clearly put, and debated with our friends'.

537 **Poly-View.**
Blantyre, Malawi: University of Malawi, 1971-, annual.
A magazine of general interest published by students of the Polytechnic in Blantyre, who also put out *Challenge* on a monthly basis.

Newspapers, Magazines, and Periodicals

538 Star.

Blantyre, Malawi, monthly.

A popular magazine geared toward Malawian women, edited by James Mwela.

539 Tsopano.

Blantyre, Malawi, 1959-61, monthly.

This news magazine was published in English in Salisbury. Its editorial policy was favourable to African independence, and it contained articles by Guy Clutton-Brock and thumbnail sketches of Malawian political figures.

540 (University publications).

Limbe, Malawi: University of Malawi.

These include *Unisport*, a monthly sports magazine; the Centre for Extension Studies' *Newsletter*; *Umodzi*, a magazine for students; and *History in Malawi*, a research bulletin of the history department, edited by Owen Kalinga.

541 Vision of Malawi.

Blantyre, Malawi: Department of Information, 1970-, quarterly.

Department of Information publication replacing *This is Malawi*. Also see *Malawi This Week*; *Facts about Malawi*; and *Malawi Calling*.

542 Youth News.

Limbe, Malawi, 1972-, quarterly.

Quarterly publication of the Malawi Young Pioneers.

Bibliographies

543 Annotated bibliography of labor in Southern Africa.
Robert B. Boeder. *Rural Africana*, no. 24 (Spring 1974),
p. 49-58.
Contains items on Malawi.

544 Books about Malawi: a select reading list.
Blantyre, Malawi: Malawi National Library Service, 1969.
23p.
A list of 250 titles, which appeared on the first anniversary of the establishment
of the Malawi National Library Service. It was intended to 'display the scope and
variety of published sources' on the country.

545 A bibliography of Malawi.
Edward E. Brown, Carol A. Fisher, John B.
Webster. Syracuse, New York: Syracuse University Press,
1965. 161p.
Contains 3,000 titles classified under twenty-four headings, and an author index,
but lacks annotations. Also see John B. Webster and Paulus Mohome, *A supple-
ment to a bibliography of Malawi* (Syracuse: Syracuse University Program of
Eastern African Studies, 1969).

**546 Audio-visual catalogue: items available in departments at
Chancellor College.**
Compiled by F. M. Chimulu. Zomba, Malawi: University
of Malawi, 1977.
A list of 377 items with some annotations, which indicate the purpose of the film,
the quality of the sound track, and the colour.

Bibliographies

547 **Education in Malawi: a bibliography.**
Jonathan M. Daube. Limbe, Malawi: University of
Malawi, 1970. 3rd ed. 15p.
Contains 212 items arranged alphabetically: journal articles, reports, government
publications, and publications in typescript.

548 **An annotated bibliography of education in Malawi.**
R. Jackson. Zomba, Malawi: University of Malawi, 1976.
57p. (Library Publication, no. 2).
The extent of the literature dealing with educational developments in Malawi is
surprisingly extensive and varied.

549 **Federalism in Rhodesia and Nyasaland.**
J. Gus Liebenow, Robert I. Rotberg. In: *Federalism in the
Commonwealth: a bibliographical commentary*, edited by
W. S. Livingstone. London: Cassell, for the Hansard
Society, 1963, p. 193-223.
Nyasaland gets only one page out of the thirty.

550 **One hundred years of Chichewa in writing, 1875-1975: a
select bibliography.**
S. M. Made, M. V. B. Mangoche Mbewe, R.
Jackson. Zomba, Malawi: University of Malawi, 1976. 87p.
Over 1,000 entries, but no annotations. When this book was compiled Jackson
was professor of education at the university; Made was chief librarian; and
Mbewe was lecturer in English.

551 **An interim bibliography of development in Malawi.**
Malawi University. Limbe, Malawi: Chancellor College
Library, 1972. 26p.
Lists items in the main library of the university; some have annotations.

552 **Nyasaland papers in the Public Record Office.**
Compiled by A. W. C. Msiska. Zomba, Malawi: University
of Malawi, 1973; Supplement, 1974. 259p.
An extremely useful index of the contents of all official correspondence between
Nyasaland and the Foreign and Colonial Offices from 1901 to 1937.

553 **Malawi.**
Steve S. Mwiyeriwa. In: *The book trade of the world. Vol.
3*, edited by S. Taubert. London: Andre Deutsch, 1979.
Also see the author's 'Printing presses and publishing in Malawi', in *African
Book Publishing Record*, vol. 4, pt. 2 (April 1978), p. 87-97. It discusses the
eighteen printing and publishing houses in the country, their publishing policies,
and book distribution agencies.

554 **List of publications deposited in the National Archives.**
National Archives. Zomba, Malawi: The Archives, 1965-,
annual.
Now called the *Malawi National Bibliography.*

555 **Political change in colonial Malawi: a bibliographical essay.**
Roger Tangri. *African Studies Bulletin*, vol. 11, pt. 3
(1969), p. 269-85.
'The purpose of this essay is to provide a guide to some of the more important
works and material concerning selected aspects of Malawi's political history during the colonial period, presenting the literature in terms of the comparative
analysis of political change in colonial Africa'.

556 **Recent trends in Central African historiography.**
A. R. Taylor. In: *Historians in tropical Africa:
Proceedings of the Leverhulm Intercollegiate History
Conference*, Salisbury: University College, 1962, p. 387-400.
This paper lists, and briefly annotates, publications concerning the history of
Central Africa which appeared between 1945 and 1960. The author remarks that
the period between 1914 and 1953 is not well documented, and this situation has
not greatly changed in recent years.

557 **The Rhodesias and Nyasaland: a guide to official
publications.**
Audrey A. Walker. Washington, D.C.: Library of
Congress, 1965. 285p.
This guide was compiled in the Library of Congress, from American sources, and
apparently without reference to the National Archives in Zomba and Salisbury or
· the Public Record Office in London, where all the basic documents are stored.

Index

The index is a single alphabetical sequence of authors (personal and corporate), titles of publications and subjects. Index entries refer both to the main items and to other works mentioned in the notes to each item. Title entries are in italics. Numeration refers to the items as numbered.

Beckman, F. von B. 392
Beef production 460
Beginnings of Nyasaland and north-eastern Rhodesia, 1859-95 119
Belcher, Sir Charles 56
Bellingham, W. 215
Benguela 126
Bennett, N. R. 175, 193
Benson, C. W. 54—56, 82
Berries, Edible 9
Bertram, C. K. R. 424
Bettison, D. G. 346, 406, 435
Bhila, H. H. K. 436
Bibliographies
Central African Federation 549, 557
Cewa literature 550
economic development 551
education 547—548
employment 543
labour 543
Malawi 544—545
official papers 552
official publications 557
political development 551, 555
Bibliography, National 554
Bibliography of Malawi 545
Bierly, E. J. 82
Big game 67, 299, 311
Big-game hunting 16, 21
Binns, B. 57—59
Biographies 34
Biology 517
Biology Teacher of Malawi Newsletter 517
Birds 8, 56, 76
aquatic 73
Nsanje 75
Birds of Nyasaland 56
Birth ceremonies 239
Tumbuka 292
Birth control 344
Bismarck, Joseph 96
Bithrey, W. B. 484
Blackmun, B. 506
Blake, W. T. 297
Blantyre 164, 232, 300, 310, 336, 346
birds 73
Chileka Airport 472
Church of St. Michael and All Angels 230
early history 182
history 1, 5, 177
life and customs 1
markets 406—407

mission 218, 226, 232, 260, 268, 447, 482, 524
mission hospitals 314
ophthalmic centre 320
servants 435
street names 176
water supply 426
Blantyre historical guide 5
Blantyre Mission 183
Blantyre missionaries: discreditable disclosures 218
Blantyre Polytechnic 537
Blantyre Urban Court 105
Blinkhorn, T. A. 419
Blood, A. G. 212
Bloomfield, K. 38, 52
Bocarro, Gaspar 306
Boeder, R. B. 187, 323, 436—437, 543
Book trades 553
Books about Malawi: a select reading list 544
Booth, Joseph 15, 243
Borden, R. W. 56
Boreholes 42
Borley, H. J. H. 424
Bowie, John 232
Brachystegia woodlands 68
Brass, L. J. 54, 60
Break-up: some economic consequences for the Rhodesias and Nyasaland 423
Brenan, J. P. M. 57, 60
Brenda-Beckman, F. von 392
Bridges, Roy 39
Brietzke, P. 382, 438
Britain
economic aid 421
Britain and Nyasaland 358
British Central Africa 124
British South Africa Company 119, 146, 157
Britten, J. 60
Brown, C. P. 407, 452
Brown, E. E. 545
Brown, H. 344
Brown, Henry 118
Brown, P. 467
Brown, R. 192
Brown, T. M. 338
Bruce, Alexander Livingstone 190
Bruwer, J. P. 262
Bua, Upper 52
Buchanan Brothers 433
Buchanan, John 2, 176, 463, 469
Budget, National 431

139

S

Map of Malawi

This map shows the more important towns and other features.

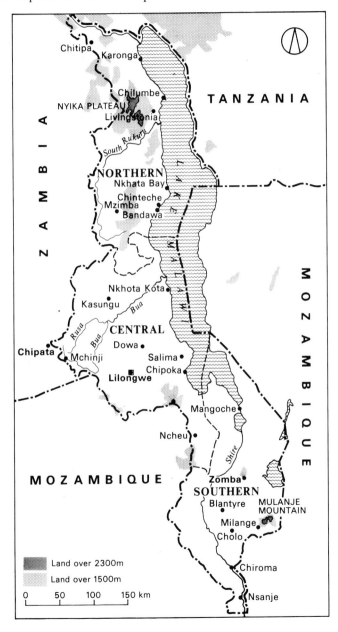